# Easy Grammar: Daily Guided

# Teaching and Review for Grade 2

*Wanda C. Phillips*

**Easy Grammar Systems**

P. O. Box 25970

Scottsdale, Arizona 85255

Printed in the United States

**www.easygrammar.com**

© 2007

# Table of Contents

**TO THE TEACHER:**

The purpose of *Easy Grammar: Daily Guided Teaching and Review for Grade 2* is to provide students with an opportunity to learn their language and to review language concepts.

Although this is a similar format to *Daily Grams* texts, this text is <u>not</u> a review text. As the title indicates, its purpose is to *TEACH and review.* **Do each lesson with your students.**

<u>FORMAT</u>:

Each lesson (day) is set up in this manner:

1. Sentence 1 will always contain capitalization errors. Please turn to page *v* to peruse the capitalization "Content and Sequence." This provides both rules covered and lessons in which each rule is introduced and/or reviewed.

2. In sentence 2 of each lesson, students will need to insert needed punctuation. It is suggested that students write this sentence or phrase and add proper punctuation. Please turn to page *vii* to peruse the punctuation "Content and Sequence." This provides both rules covered and lessons in which each rule is introduced and/or reviewed.

3. Sentence 3 will be TEACHING and/or REVIEW of various concepts. (After DAY 90, this is expanded to include a #4.) Please turn to page *ix* to peruse the "Content and Sequence" for grammar and other concepts. This not only provides the various concepts included but also tells you in which lessons the concept occurs.

4. The last part of each lesson is sentence combining. In DAYS 1-90, this will be #4; in DAYS 91-180, this will be #5. Using sentences given, students will write one higher-level sentence. This process helps students learn new ways of expressing thoughts, vary sentences, and improve the quality of their writing. (If you feel that the sentences are too difficult for your students, you may delete parts or create your own sentences for this activity.) You have been given at least one possible answer. Often there are more.

## TO THE TEACHER:

*This text may seem too easy at the beginning. If you peruse the last few pages, you may think that those lessons are too advanced for a second grader. Don't be concerned!! The lessons are spiraled and gradually increase in complexity.*

1. Read the **"Ideas and Suggestions for Effective Teaching"** before you begin each lesson. Be creative and use your own ideas as well!

2. This text is **reproducible** for student use (not for commercial use). **Workbooks** are also available. Although this text has been designed for second grade students, some teachers may find it helpful to use with older students, especially second-language students.

3. **DO EACH LESSON ORALLY WITH STUDENTS.** It is ideal to make a **transparency** so that students can follow along easily. This also incorporates both **visual** and **auditory** sensory learning.

4. **Solicit much student response**.

5. **Try to use examples that relate to your students.** If you are teaching capitalization for names of businesses, for example, solicit answers for local restaurants, grocery stores, and other places familiar to your students.

6.  **Be enthusiastic about your teaching of the language!**

7.  As one progresses through this text, some of the sentences become longer and/or more complex.  This may necessitate an adaptation to students' needs.

# CAPITALIZATION
## Content and Sequence
### Daily Guided Teaching and Review for Grade 2

*Numbers after each category indicate DAYS (lessons) where that concept is introduced or reviewed.*

**ABBREVIATION** (Includes Initials):   2, 15, 26, 28, 67, 87, 108, 117, 128, 144, 159, 164, 171, 173

**BUSINESS:**   22, 25-26, 33, 41, 43, 45, 63, 80, 86, 89, 126, 134, 137, 173

**CLOSING of a LETTER:**   65-66, 69, 71, 103, 124, 135, 142, 149

**CLUB/ORGANIZATION/TEAM:**   49, 78-79, 81, 101, 114, 116, 167

**DAY of the WEEK:**   3, 7, 9, 17-18, 42, 51, 55, 70, 83, 101, 131, 149, 172

**EVENTS:**   120, 121, 132, 170, 178

**GEOGRAPHIC PLACES:**
Bay:   119, 171
Beach:   118, 127, 131
Bridge:   123
Cape:   128
Cavern:   163
Continent:   165
Country:   10-12, 68, 76, 96-97, 99, 107, 129, 136, 151
Creek:   29, 71
Dam:   176
Forest:   156
Garden(s):   109
Island(s):   84, 90, 115
Lake:   (29), 30, 68, 104, 115, 141, 152        ( ) Rule stated but not reinforced in sentence.
Mountain(s):   35-36, 61, 102, 125
Ocean:   (29), 31, 104, 131           ( ) Rule stated but not reinforced in sentence.
Park:   39, 42, 98, 105, 108, 169
Pond:   (29)        ( ) Rule stated but not reinforced in sentence.
River:   (29), 34, 70, 85, 161        ( ) Rule stated but not reinforced in sentence.
Sea:   (29)        ( ) Rule stated but not reinforced in sentence.
State:   10, 14, 18, 30, 43, 46, 61, 64, 67, 72, 80, 82, 102, 105, 109, 119, 128, 143-144, 152, 155-156, 166, 169
Town/City:   10, 14, 47, 62, 67, 105, 109, 120-121, 144, 155, 166, 168, 176
Waterfall:   143

**GREETING of a FRIENDLY LETTER:**·  53-54, 69, 71, 103, 124, 135, 142, 149, 166

**HOLIDAY/SPECIAL DAY:**   20-21, 24, 40, 64, 85, 98, 100, 111, 148, 177

**LANGUAGE:**   73, 76, 95, 131, 160, 168

**MONTH:**   8-9, 17, 24, 40, 44, 48, 51, 55, 70, 90, 96, 106-107, 118, 148-149, 163, 166, 168, 177

**NAMES of PEOPLE:**   1-2, 5, 11, 16, 19, 26, 28, 31-32, 38-39, 44, 47, 50, 53-54, 62-63, 65-67, 69, 71-72, 74-75, 79, 86-87, 93-94, 96, 99-100, 102-103, 108-110, 117, 122, 124-125, 128, 130, 135, 138, 141-142, 144-145, 149, 151-152, 155, 157-162, 164, 166, 171, 173, 178, 180

# PUNCTUATION

## Content and Sequence

*Daily Guided Teaching and Review for Grade 2*

*Numbers after each category indicate DAYS (lessons) that concept is introduced or reviewed.*

### APOSTROPHE:
Contraction:  18, 28-29, 39, 42, 47, 48, 59-61, 65, 71, 76, 78, 90, 92, 100, 102, 115, 120, 122, 128, 130, 132, 137, 150-152, 155, 158, 162, 171, 173

Plural Possessive:  72-73, 85-86, 89, 98, 107, 116, 145, 166

Singular Possessive:  34-35, 37, 41, 45, 52, 56-58, 64, 66-67, 79, 85-86, 89, 94, 98, 101, 115-117, 120, 125, 130, 132, 144, 149, 158-159, 162, 176, 179-180

### COLON:
Time:  91, 93, 132, 137, 140, 161, 175

### COMMA:
Address Within Sentence *(I live at 1 Lu Lane, Reno, Nevada.)*:  88, 108, 155, 157, 178, 180

Closing of a Letter:  90, 105, 161, 163

Date *(January 1, 2000)*:  16, 23, 71, 80-81, 94-95, 97, 118, 127, 130, 149, 161

Date *(Monday, January 1)*:  12, 13, 17, 36, 44, 81, 93, 97, 127-128, 133, 140, 143, 161, 163

Descriptive Adjectives (Two):  165, 168

Greeting of a Friendly letter:  53, 63, 90, 104, 161, 163

Introductory Word:  25, 26, 33, 39, 44, 48, 59, 78, 102, 109, 137, 158, 161

Items in a Series:  43, 51, 55, 70, 106, 112, 113, 117, 124, 126, 131, 159, 171, 176

Noun of Direct Address:  47, 50, 54, 77, 139, 141, 145, 152, 173

Quotation Marks:  110, 147, 148, 164, 171, 173, 179

Town/City with State *(Conway, SC)*:  19, 20, 32, 46, 82, 87, 91, 96, 111, 114, 123, 136, 138, 142, 150, 155, 157, 161, 163, 165, 178, 180

### EXCLAMATION POINT:
Exclamatory Sentence:  7, 11, 29, 65, 101, 105, 119, 122, 151, 164, 179

Interjection:  22, 29, 65, 101, 105, 119, 122, 151, 164

### HYPHEN:
Number:  56, 133, 135

### PERIOD:
Abbreviation:  4-5, 8-10, 14, 15, 21, 26-31, 33, 38, 40, 49, 71, 80, 88, 90-91, 93, 97, 108, 111, 114, 117, 123, 127, 129, 133-134, 138, 140, 143, 146, 149, 156, 159, 160-161, 163, 165, 173-175

Outline:  153, 175

Sentence ending:  1, 10, 12, 16, 20, 25-26, 28, 33, 38, 41-44, 46, 48-49, 51, 55-56, 5962, 70-71 76, 78-79, 88, 90-94, 97, 102, 109, 112, 115, 124, 125-128, 130-132, 135, 137, 140, 143-144, 147, 149-150, 152, 155, 157-159, 161, 163, 165-166, 168, 175-176

### QUESTON MARK:  2, 3, 6, 9, 13-14, 18, 47, 50, 54, 74, 77, 96, 99-100, 106, 110, 113, 134, 139, 141, 145, 148, 171, 173

## QUOTATION MARKS:

## UNDERLINING:

## DO NOT PLACE A COMMA:

## DO NOT PLACE A PERIOD:

# GRAMMAR AND OTHER CONCEPTS

## Content and Sequence

*Daily Guided Teaching and Review for Grade 2*

*Numbers after each category indicate DAYS (lessons) where that concept is introduced or reviewed.*

**ADJECTIVES:**
    Adjective or Adverb Usage:  165
    Degrees:  148, 153, 178
    Descriptive:  26, 32, 39, 51, 77, 95, 97, 105, 113, 115, 121, 140, 152, 166, (170*), 174, 178
    Limiting:  77, 113, 124, 146, 152, 170, 174

**ADVERBS:**
    Adverb or Adjective Usage:  165
    Double Negatives:  96, 99, 104, 129, 158, 168, 177
    How:  49, 61, 74, 79, 94, 131, 148, 174
    To What Extent:  161, 175
    When:  79, 100, 110, 131, 148, 156, 174
    Where:  79, 131, 135, 148, 156, 174

**COMPOUND WORDS:**  24, 36, 69, 102, 122, 142

**CONJUNCTIONS (Coordinating):**  63, 68, 114, 153, 157, 162

**DICTIONARY SKILLS:**
    Alphabetizing:  1, 12, 22, 60, 94, 105, 109, 134, 145, 177
    Guide Words:  46, 75, 112, 141, 144, 165
    Reading an Entry:  56, 81
    Syllables:  41, 72, 73, 106, 119, 132, 167

**DIFFICULT WORDS:**
    It's/Its:  113, 151
    They're/Their/There:  112-113, 127, 150, 177
    To/Two/Too:  120, 128, 151, 177
    You're/Your:  138

**FRIENDLY LETTERS:**
    Letter Parts:  160, 163

**INTERJECTIONS:**  67, 88, 136, 156

**NOUNS:**
    Common/Proper:  126, 129, 138, 147, 154, 173
    Identification:  2, 6, 9, 11, 13, 23, 31, 44, 62, 101, 114, 141, 151
    Plurals:  20, 21, 29, 35, 47, 93, 97, 120, 124, 142, 145, 154, 159, 164, 170, 175
    Possessives:  135

**PREFIXES/ROOTS/SUFFIXES:**  8, 18, 34, 40, 52, 53, 55, 80, 109, 111, 134, 137, 139, 144, 172, 176

*Parentheses (  ) designate a relationship to another category, also.

## CAPITALIZATION:

**Capitalize a person's name.**

1. nancy    Nancy

## PUNCTUATION:

**Place a period at the end of a statement.**

2. I like you    because you are kind.

## ALPHABETIZING:

Write these words in alphabetical order.

3. girl    boy    dog

a) boy

b) dog

c) girl

## SENTENCE COMBINING:

4. That ball is round.
   That ball is green.

That ball is round and that ball is green.

**DAY 2**

**CAPITALIZATION:**

**Capitalize initials with names.**

Example: Sarah **C**. Hops

1. bob h. smith    Bob H. Smith

**PUNCTUATION:**

**Place a question mark (?) at the end of a question.**

2. Are you going ___to work?___

**PARTS OF SPEECH:    NOUNS**

Write the word in the sentence that names a <u>thing</u>.

3. Your kite is big.    ___Kite___

**SENTENCE COMBINING:**

4. My shirt is torn.
   My shirt is red.
   ___My red shirt is___
   ___torn___

**CAPITALIZATION:**

**Capitalize the names of the days of the week.**

1.  tuesday

**PUNCTUATION:**

2.  Is this your pen _____

**RHYMING WORDS:**

**Words that rhyme end in the same sound.**

Example:  p**in** - w**in**

3.  A word that rhymes with <u>all</u> is _____.

**SENTENCE COMBINING:**

4.  Bob likes peanut butter.
    Bob likes honey.

_____

_____

_____

## CAPITALIZATION:

**Capitalize the first word of a sentence.**

1.  her toy fell on the floor.

## PUNCTUATION:

**Place a period after <u>Mr.</u> and <u>Mrs.</u>, but do not place a period after <u>Miss</u> when you see it or write it.**

Examples:   Mr. and Mrs. Beem
Miss Beem

2.  Mr Jones    _____

## SUBJECT:

**The subject tells <u>who</u> or <u>what</u> the sentence is about.**

*Who* is the sentence about?

3.  Sam eats fast.

_____

## SENTENCE COMBINING:

4.  Jill jumped up.
Ken jumped up.

_____

_____

**CAPITALIZATION:**

1.  his best friend is joe.

**PUNCTUATION:**

2.  Mrs Smith _____

**PARTS OF SPEECH:   VERBS**

> **The verb tells what <u>is</u> or what <u>happens</u> in a sentence.**

> What word in the sentence tells what Sam does?

3.  Sam eats fast.     _____

**SENTENCE COMBINING:**

4.  His car is new.
    His car is blue.

    _____

    _____

    _____

**DAY 6**

**CAPITALIZATION:**

**Capitalize the pronoun I.**

1. Tom and i

**PUNCTUATION:**

2. May I go _____

**PARTS OF SPEECH:   NOUNS**

**A noun names a person.**

Write the noun that names a person in the following sentence.

3. My friend is nice.   _____

**SENTENCE COMBINING:**

4. His hair is black.
   His hair is shiny.

   _____

   _____

   _____

**CAPITALIZATION:**

1. may i come next monday?

**PUNCTUATION:**

**An exclamation mark (!) is used at the end of a sentence that shows excitement.**

Example:   We can go!

Use the end mark that shows excitement in the following sentence.

2. We won   _____

**PARTS OF SPEECH:   VERBS**

**A verb tells what <u>happens</u> or what <u>is</u> in a sentence.**

Choose the verb in the following sentence.  The verb tells what the dog does.

3. Our dog chews his bone.   _____

**SENTENCE COMBINING:**

4. Peter ate an apple.
   The apple was red.

_____

_____

**CAPITALIZATION:**

**Capitalize months of the year.**

1. april

**PUNCTUATION:**

2. Mr and Mrs Little _____

**PREFIXES/ROOTS/SUFFIXES:**

**Some words are made by adding an ending called a suffix.**

Example:   talk   +   ing   =   talking

(root)      **(suffix)**

3. wish + ing =   _____

**SENTENCE COMBINING:**

4. Tammy threw a ball.
   The ball is large.

   _____

   _____

   _____

**CAPITALIZATION:**

1.  sunday, february 10

**PUNCTUATION:**

2.  Did Miss Barnes leave

_____

**PARTS OF SPEECH:   NOUNS**

**A noun names a person, place, or thing.**

Write the noun that names a <u>place</u> in the following sentence.

3.  Are you going to the mall?          _____

**SENTENCE COMBINING:**

4.  Josh ran to the store.
    He ran fast.

_____

_____

_____

**DAY 10**

## CAPITALIZATION:

**Capitalize the name of a town (city), state, or country.**

Examples:   city  =  **N**ew **Y**ork **C**ity

state  =  **F**lorida

country  =  **U**nited **S**tates of **A**merica

1.   The town (city) where I live is _____.

*Mister*

## PUNCTUATION:

*Doctor*
*Dr. Smith*

2.   Mr and Mrs Simms are here today

_____

## SYNONYMS/ANTONYMS/HOMONYMS:

**Homonyms are words that sound alike but are spelled differently.**

Example:   hi  -  high

3.   The homonym for <u>sale</u> is _____.

## SENTENCE COMBINING:

4.   Kim hit the ball.
     She hit it hard.

_____

_____

**CAPITALIZATION:**

1. my family and i live in america*.

   *name of a country

**PUNCTUATION:**

**An exclamation mark (!) is used at the end of a sentence that shows excitement.**

2. You are the winner _____

**PARTS OF SPEECH:   NOUNS**

**A noun names a place.**

Write a noun that names a <u>place</u> in the following sentence.

3. We went to the park. _____

**SENTENCE COMBINING:**

4. The baby laughed.
   The baby threw a rattle.

   _____

   _____

   _____

**DAY 12**

**CAPITALIZATION:**

1.  their aunt lives in the country of mexico.

**PUNCTUATION:**

   **Place a comma between a day and a month.**

   Example:   Tuesday, September 21

2.  My birthday is Thursday March 12

_____

**ALPHABETIZING:**

   Write these words in alphabetical order.

3.  sock      list      trip

   a)  _____

   b)  _____

   c)  _____

**SENTENCE COMBINING:**

4.  That hill is high.
    Some people climb that hill.

_____

_____

## CAPITALIZATION:

**Capitalize the name of a street, avenue, road, lane, way, boulevard, highway, or freeway.**

Examples:    **A**coma **A**venue

**P**apago **F**reeway

1.  I live on (name of street or road) _____.

## PUNCTUATION:

2.  Does school start on Monday September 7

_____

## PARTS OF SPEECH:    NOUNS

**A noun names a person, place, or thing.**

Write the noun that names a <u>person</u> in the following sentence.

3.  My dad is very funny.    _____

## SENTENCE COMBINING:

4.  A dog barked at us.
    The dog chased us, too.

_____

_____

**DAY 14**

## CAPITALIZATION:

1. they live in austin*, texas**.

*name of a city
**name of a state

## PUNCTUATION:

**Some words can be shortened.  A period is added.**

Examples:   A.  Doctor = Dr.        C.  inch = in.

B.  Street = St.        D.  Carol Zoe  = Carol Z.

2. Is Dr Evans nice

_____

## SYNONYMS/ANTONYMS/HOMONYMS:

**Homonyms are words that sound alike but are spelled differently.**

Example:   sea  -  see

3. The homonym for <u>buy</u> is _____.

## SENTENCE COMBINING:

4. A paper is lying on the floor.
   It is Barry's.

_____

_____

_____

## CAPITALIZATION:

### Capitalize titles with names.

Examples:   Dr. Mary A. Owens

Uncle Rick

1. the nurse gave dr. lipton a folder.

## PUNCTUATION:

2. 12 Elm St

_____

## SUBJECT:

### A subject tells <u>who</u> or <u>what</u> the sentence is about.

Write the subject of this sentence.

3. A lizard crawled away.  _____

## SENTENCE COMBINING:

4. The baby cried.
   The baby was hungry.

_____

_____

_____

## CAPITALIZATION:

1.  today aunt jane will read to me.

## PUNCTUATION:

**Place a comma after the day in a date.**

Example:    January 9, 2000

2.  Becky was born October 21 1989

_____

## PARTS OF SPEECH:    VERBS

**A verb tells what <u>happens</u> or what <u>is</u>.  If something has already happened, you usually add <u>ed</u> to the end of the verb.**

Write the verb that tells <u>what happened</u> in this sentence.

3.  The lizard crawled away.     (Hint:  What did the lizard do?)

_____

## SENTENCE COMBINING:

4.  The dish is red.
    The dish is cracked.

_____

_____

## CAPITALIZATION:

1. friday, july 10

## PUNCTUATION:

**Place a comma between the name of a day and the name of a month.**

2. Sunday May 10 _____

## PARTS OF SPEECH:   VERBS

**A contraction is made by joining two words but leaving out a letter or some letters.  Place an apostrophe ( ' ) where the letter or letters have been left out.**

Example:   has not  =  hasn't   (Can you see that the o has
been left out?)

Write the contraction.

3. is not   ___isn't___

## SENTENCE COMBINING:

4. Jack drank a glass of water.
   Jack was thirsty.

   _____

   _____

   _____

**DAY 18**

## CAPITALIZATION:

1. on tuesday i will go to nevada*.

*name of a state

## PUNCTUATION:

**Place an apostrophe ( ' ) where a letter or letters have been left out of a word.**

Examples:   was not  =  wasn't          I am  =  I'm

2. Isnt Jenny here

_____


## PREFIXES/ROOTS/SUFFIXES:

**Some words are made by adding an ending called a suffix.**

Example:   jump  +  **ed**  =  jumped
          (root)      (suffix)

3. push  +  ed  =  _____


## SENTENCE COMBINING:

4. Cindy has a wagon.
   It is purple.
   It is new.

_____

_____

_____

**CAPITALIZATION:**

1. linda and grandpa wells went fishing.

**PUNCTUATION:**

   **Place a comma between the name of a town (city) and state.**

   Example:   Dayton, Ohio

2. Kingman Arizona   _____

   (city)    (state)

**PARTS OF SPEECH:   VERBS**

   **A contraction is made by joining two words but leaving out a letter or some of the letters.  Place an apostrophe ( ' ) where the letter or letters have been left out.**

   Example:   we are  =  we're

3. The contraction for <u>have not</u> is _____.

**SENTENCE COMBINING:**

4. Mary tickles her brother.
   Mary also tickles her sister.

   _____

   _____

   _____

**DAY 20**

## CAPITALIZATION:

**Capitalize the name of a special day or a holiday.**

Example:   Flag **D**ay

1.  i made a card for valentine's day.

## PUNCTUATION:

2.  Ken lives in Topeka Kansas
              (city)     (state)

_____

## PARTS OF SPEECH:   NOUNS

**Plural means more than one.**
**Most plurals are made by adding s to the word.**

Example:   one dog   /   two dog**s**

Write the plural of these words.

3.  a)  girl - _____          b)  car - _____

## SENTENCE COMBINING:

4.  A clown threw three balls.
    He threw them up in the air.

    _____

    _____

## CAPITALIZATION:

1.  does your family have turkey on thanksgiving*?

    *name of a holiday

## PUNCTUATION:

2.  Miss Sarah P Kent _____

## PARTS OF SPEECH:   NOUNS

> **Plural means more than one.**
> **Most plurals are made by adding s to the word.**
> **If a word ends in sh, add es to the word to make it plural.**

> Example:   one dish  /  many dish**es**

Write the plural of these words.

3.  a) thumb - _____    b) wish - _____

## SENTENCE COMBINING:

4.  His kitten is a week old.
    His kitten is white.

    _____

    _____

    _____

**CAPITALIZATION:**

**Capitalize the name of a store or other business.**

1. they went to poppa's pizza*.

*name of a business

**PUNCTUATION:**

**Place an exclamation mark ( ! ) after a word or phrase (group of words) that shows excitement.**

Example: Yippee!

2. Wow _____

**ALPHABETIZING:**

Write these words in alphabetical order.

3. father    egg    ham

a) _____

b) _____

c) _____

**SENTENCE COMBINING:**

4. Tom walked home.
   Sue walked home.

_____

_____

**CAPITALIZATION:**

1. her friend lives on tulip avenue.


**PUNCTUATION:**

2. April 10  2015  _____


**PARTS OF SPEECH:   NOUNS**

   **A noun names a person, place, or thing.**

   Write the noun that names a <u>thing</u> in the following sentence.

3. That pan is dirty.  _____


**SENTENCE COMBINING:**

4. Paco stubbed his toe.
   Paco yelled.

   _____

   _____

   _____

**DAY 24**

## CAPITALIZATION:

1.  is fathers' day* near the end of june?

    *name of a special day

## PUNCTUATION:

2.  Sunday November 10

   _____


## COMPOUNDS:

   **A compound word is made by joining two regular words.**

   Example:   snow  +  man  =  **snowman**

3.  The compound word for <u>fire</u> + <u>man</u> is _____.

## SENTENCE COMBINING:

4.  A tiny baby opened his eyes.
    He waved his arms.

   _____

   _____

   _____

## CAPITALIZATION:

1. the new store is called pet palace.

## PUNCTUATION:

**Place a comma after <u>No</u> or <u>Yes</u> at the beginning of a sentence.**

Example:   Yes, we want that.

2. No I am not going

_____


## SYNONYMS/ANTONYMS/HOMONYMS:

**A synonym is a word with almost the same meaning as another word.**

Example:   big  -  large

3. A synonym for <u>street</u> is _____.

## SENTENCE COMBINING:

4. Brad went home.
   His sister went home, also.

_____

_____

_____

**DAY 26**

**CAPITALIZATION:**

1.  mr. flogg works for aero airlines*.

    *name of a business

**PUNCTUATION:**

2.  Yes Mrs Eller voted

_____

**PARTS OF SPEECH:   ADJECTIVES**

**Adjectives are describing words.**

**Adjectives that describe usually tell <u>what kind</u>.**

Write the adjective that tells <u>what kind</u> of bird in the following sentence.

3.  We saw a tiny bird.   _____

**SENTENCE COMBINING:**

4.  That pan is full of hot water.
    That pan is a frying pan.

_____

_____

_____

**CAPITALIZATION:**

1. in march i like to fly a kite.

**PUNCTUATION:**

Match the word and its abbreviation.

2. _____ mt.          A.  street

   _____ st.          B.  foot

   _____ ft.          C.  mountain

**SUBJECT:**

**The subject is <u>who</u> or <u>what</u> the sentence is about.**

Find the subject.

3.  My brother runs slowly.     _____

**SENTENCE COMBINING:**

4.  The wagon is blue.
    Mary pulls her sister in the wagon.

    _____

    _____

    _____

**DAY 28**

**CAPITALIZATION:**

1. does mr. sparks live on elm street?

**PUNCTUATION:**

**Place an apostrophe ( ' ) where a letter or letters have been left out of a word.**

Examples:   he is  =  he's          I have  =  I've

2. Mrs Argus isnt leaving today

_____

**PARTS OF SPEECH:   VERBS**

**The verb tells <u>what is</u> or <u>what happens</u> (<u>does</u>).**

Find the verb.

3. My brother runs slowly.     (Hint:  What does my brother do?)

_____

**SENTENCE COMBINING:**

4. We will eat hot dogs for lunch.
   We will eat beans for lunch, too.

_____

_____

_____

## CAPITALIZATION:

**Capitalize the name of an ocean, sea, lake, river, creek, pond, or the name of any other body of water.**

1. our friend lives near skunk creek.

## PUNCTUATION:

**Place a period after the abbreviation of a month.**

Example:   October  =  Oct.

2. Yeah  Were taking a Nov vacation

_____

## PARTS OF SPEECH:   NOUNS

**Plural means more than one.**
**Most plurals are made by adding <u>s</u> to the word.**
**If a word ends in <u>sh</u> or <u>ch</u>, add <u>es</u>.**

Write the plural of the following words.

3.    a)  bug - _____

   b)  ditch - _____

   c)  eyelash - _____

## SENTENCE COMBINING:

4. Jenny fell.
   She scraped her knee.

_____

_____

**CAPITALIZATION:**

1.  my favorite place is big clear lake in wisconsin*.

    *name of a state

**PUNCTUATION:**

**Place a period after the abbreviation for directions.**

Examples:  North = N.      East = E.

South = S.      West = W.

2.  272 S Central Avenue

_____

**SYNONYMS/ANTONYMS/HOMONYMS:**

**Antonyms are words that have opposite meanings.**

Example:  up  -  down

3.  An antonym for <u>hot</u> is _____.

**SENTENCE COMBINING:**

4.  Their street is wide.
    Their street is paved.

_____

_____

## CAPITALIZATION:

1. mary lives near the pacific ocean.

## PUNCTUATION:

2. 1909 E Flower Lane

_____

## PARTS OF SPEECH:   NOUNS

**A noun names a person, place, or thing.**

Write the two nouns that name <u>things</u>.

3. They have a car and two bikes.   _____   _____

## SENTENCE COMBINING:

4. That bear is eating berries.
   That bear is also eating honey.

_____

_____

_____

**DAY 32**

## CAPITALIZATION:

1.  i will go to dr. fisk's office soon.

## PUNCTUATION:

2.  Tampa  Florida  _____

    (city)   (state)

## PARTS OF SPEECH:   ADJECTIVES

**Adjectives are describing words.**
**Adjectives that describe usually tell <u>what kind</u>.**

Find the adjective that tells <u>what kind</u>.

3.  A paper bag is on the table.   _____ bag

## SENTENCE COMBINING:

4.  Tate raced his friends.
    Tate won.

    _____

    _____

    _____

## CAPITALIZATION:

1.  her dad works for bell company*.

    *name of a business

## PUNCTUATION:

2.  Yes Jane lives at 6003 N Oak Trail

_____

## PARTS OF SPEECH:   VERBS

**A contraction is made by joining two words but leaving out
a letter or some letters.  Place an apostrophe ( ' ) where the letter
or letters have been left out.**

Example:   do not  =  don't   (Can you see that the <u>o</u> has been
left out?)

Write the contraction.

3.  are not  =  _____

## SENTENCE COMBINING:

4.  Their horse likes carrots.
    Their horse likes apples and hay.

_____

_____

_____

**DAY 34**

**CAPITALIZATION:**

1.  you should see the mississippi river.

**PUNCTUATION:**

**We own many things.**
**To show that someone owns something, write the person's name and add 's.**

Example:  a kite that Tammy owns  =  Tammy**'s** kite

2.  _____'s _____

(your name)                          (your favorite toy or pet)

**PREFIXES/ROOTS/SUFFIXES:**

**A root is any word without an important part added at the beginning or a part added at the end.**

Examples:  walking     =     **walk**     +     ing

unhappy     =     un     +     **happy**

3.  The root of <u>showing</u> is _____.

**SENTENCE COMBINING:**

4.  Ricky can't go.
Lucy can't go either.

_____

_____

## CAPITALIZATION:

**Capitalize the name(s) of mountains.**

Example: **R**ocky **M**ountains

1. have you been to camelback mountain?

## PUNCTUATION:

2. shells belonging to Pat = _____ shells

## PARTS OF SPEECH:   NOUNS

**Plural means more than one.**
**Most plurals are made by adding s to the word.**
**If a word ends in sh, ch, s, x, or z, add es to make the plural.**

Examples:   one basket  -  two basket**s**

a box  =  four box**es**

Write the plural of these words.

3. a) rug - _____        b) bus - _____

## SENTENCE COMBINING:

4. This rose is pink.
   It has a long stem.

_____

_____

**DAY 36**

**CAPITALIZATION:**

1. we went to mt. shasta.

**PUNCTUATION:**

2. Monday  August 27  _____

**COMPOUND WORDS:**

**A compound word is formed by joining two regular words.**

Example:  dog  +  house  =  **doghouse**

3. The compound word for <u>drive</u> + <u>way</u> is _____.

**SENTENCE COMBINING:**

4. My mom's friend drives slowly.
   He also drives carefully.

   _____

   _____

   _____

**CAPITALIZATION:**

**Capitalize the name of a school.**

Example:   **P**ine **E**lementary **S**chool

1.   next week i will go to hilltop school.

**PUNCTUATION:**

**To show that one animal or one "thing" owns something, add 's.**

Examples:   a cat**'s** dish

one desk**'s** legs

2.   a tail of a dog = a _____ tail

**PARTS OF SPEECH:   VERBS**

**A verb tells what is or what happens in a sentence.**

What is the verb in the following sentence?

3.   Tim sings loudly.   _____

**SENTENCE COMBINING:**

4.   This paper is yellow.
     This paper is torn.

_____

_____

**DAY 38**

**CAPITALIZATION:**

1.  does kent live on copper lane?

**PUNCTUATION:**

2.  Dr and Mrs Potts were here in Dec for a week

_____

**SYNONYMS/ANTONYMS/HOMONYMS:**

**A synonym is a word with almost the same meaning as another word.**

Example:   high   -   tall

3.  A synonym for <u>little</u> is _____.

**SENTENCE COMBINING:**

4.  Kala is happy.
    Kala has won a spelling bee.

_____

_____

_____

## CAPITALIZATION:

**Capitalize the name of a park.**

1.  the harris family is going to briar park.

## PUNCTUATION:

2.  Yes I m glad you came

_____

## PARTS OF SPEECH:   ADJECTIVES

**Adjectives are describing words.**
**Adjectives that describe usually tell <u>what kind</u>.**

Find two adjectives that describe <u>nail</u> in the following sentence.

3.  An old, rusty nail is on the floor.   _____   _____

## SENTENCE COMBINING:

4.  Lulu is in the band.
    Lulu is also in the chorus.

_____

_____

_____

**CAPITALIZATION:**

1.  is easter in april?

**PUNCTUATION:**

Match the word and its abbreviation:

2.  _____ Ln.          A. yard

    _____ E.           B. East

    _____ yd.          C. Mountain

    _____ Mt.          D. Lane

**PREFIXES/ROOTS/SUFFIXES:**

**A root is a word that does not have a prefix** (part added at the beginning) **or a suffix** (part added at the end).

Examples:   unpack   =   un   +   **pack**
                                              **(root)**

                  dogs   =   **dog**   +   s
                              **(root)**

3.  The root of <u>watching</u> is _____.

**SENTENCE COMBINING:**

4.  Paco gave me a yo-yo.
    He gave one to Anna, too.

    _____

    _____

## CAPITALIZATION:

**Capitalize the name of a business.**

1.  her mother works for westways airlines*.

    *name of a business

## PUNCTUATION:

2.  Scotts dad is a dentist

_____

## DICTIONARY:   SYLLABLES

**Words have different units of sound.**
**Some words say just one sound.  These are called one-syllable words.**

　　　　　　　Examples:    bee        cat        dust        log

3.  Write a one-syllable word: _____

## SENTENCE COMBINING:

4.  Patty jumps rope.
    She jumps rope nearly every day.

_____

_____

**CAPITALIZATION:**

1.  she went to linnwood park on tuesday.

**PUNCTUATION:**

> **Do not place a comma between two items in a series if *and*, *or*, or *but* separates them.**

> Example:   girls and boys

2.  Their skates arent blue and red

_____

**RHYMING:**

> **Words that rhyme end in the same sound.**

> Example:   **lid - hid**

3.  Write a word that rhymes with <u>cat</u>.   _____

**SENTENCE COMBINING:**

4.  A bunny hopped toward me.
    The bunny was white.

_____

_____

_____

## CAPITALIZATION:

1. tot toy store* is in ohio**.

    *name of a business        **name of a state

## PUNCTUATION:

**Do not place a comma between two items in a series.**

Example:   pizza and cola

**Place a comma between more than two items in a series.
Do not place a comma after the last item.**

Example:   I like peanuts, popcorn, or pretzels for a snack.

2. Nan ate fish beans and rice for dinner

_____

## PARTS OF SPEECH:   VERBS

**A contraction is made by joining two words but leaving out
a letter or some letters.  Place an apostrophe ( ' ) where the letter
or letters have been left out.**

Example:   she is  =  she's

Write the contraction.

3. they are  =  _____

## SENTENCE COMBINING:

4. The rug is smooth.
   The rug is green.

_____

_____

**DAY 44**

## CAPITALIZATION:

1.  in february, dr. lisper will retire.

## PUNCTUATION:

2.  No today is not Friday May 15

_____

## PARTS OF SPEECH:   NOUNS

**A noun names a person, place, or thing.**

Write the noun that tells a <u>place</u> in the following sentence.

3.  He went to the beach.  _____

## SENTENCE COMBINING:

4.  Grandma plays golf.
    Grandma swims and goes to college, too.

_____

_____

_____

**CAPITALIZATION:**

1.  our uncle owns rooster restaurant*.

    *name of a business

**PUNCTUATION:**

2.  a truck that Andy owns = _____ truck

**SUBJECTS:**

**The subject is <u>who</u> or <u>what</u> a sentence is about.**

Underline the subject.

3.  That chair is broken.

**SENTENCE COMBINING:**

4.  Tate fell down a step.
    Tate hurt his knee.

    _____

    _____

    _____

## CAPITALIZATION:

**Capitalize the name of a hospital.**

Example:   John **C**. **L**incoln **H**ospital

1.  is hanover hospital in pennsylvania*?

*name of a state

## PUNCTUATION:

2.  Their brother and sister went to Rutland Vermont

_____

## DICTIONARY:   GUIDE WORDS

**At the top of every dictionary page are two words.
These are called guide words.**

Example:   **ball**                **box**

<u>Ball</u> is the first word on the page.
<u>Box</u> is the last word on the page.

3.  Will <u>bell</u> be found on a page with guide words <u>ball</u> and <u>box</u>?   _____

## SENTENCE COMBINING:

4.   Jack's mom wanted a turtle.
     She bought a lizard.

_____

_____

_____

## CAPITALIZATION:

1.  has aunt betty been to rome*?

    *name of a city

## PUNCTUATION:

**Place a comma after a person spoken to.**

Examples:  Matt, let's play.          Let's play, Matt.

2.  Barbara arent you ready

_____

## PARTS OF SPEECH:    NOUNS

**Plural means more than one.  Most plurals are made by adding s to the word.  If a word ends in sh or ch, add es to form the plural.**

Examples:          one goat / two goat**s**
                   one flash / two flash**es**
                   one punch / two punch**es**

Write the plural of the following words.

3.  a)  church - _____    c)  dash - _____

    b)  tire - _____

## SENTENCE COMBINING:

4.  Jana wants a pet.
    I want a pet, too.

_____

_____

**DAY 48**

## CAPITALIZATION:

1.  in august, he left harper hospital.

## PUNCTUATION:

2.  Yes I ll take one

_____

## PARTS OF SPEECH:   VERBS

**Verbs tell what <u>is</u> or what <u>happens</u> in a sentence.**

Write the verb.  (What word tells what Mike does?)

3.    Mike paints houses.    _____

## SENTENCE COMBINING:

4.    The ground is soft.
      It is muddy and brown.

_____

_____

_____

**CAPITALIZATION:**

**Capitalize the names of sports teams.**

Example:   **G**reen **B**ay **P**ackers

1.   we like the chicago cubs*.

   *name of a baseball team

**PUNCTUATION:**

2.   Miss Ann K Cline will drive

_____

**PARTS OF SPEECH:   ADVERBS**

**Some adverbs tell <u>how</u>.  They usually end in <u>ly</u>.**
**Adverbs that tell *how* usually help to explain the verb.**

Example:   Tate draws neatly.  (Neatly tells *how* Tate draws.)

Find the adverb that tells <u>how</u> Pam plays.

3.   Pam plays quietly.   _____

**SENTENCE COMBINING:**

4.   Our team won!
   It is a baseball team.

_____

_____

## CAPITALIZATION:

**Do not capitalize the seasons of the year.**

Examples:    spring              autumn *or* fall

summer           winter

1.  next spring i will see uncle todd.

## PUNCTUATION:

2.  Brad may Don and I come with you

_____

## PARTS OF SPEECH:   VERBS

**A contraction is made by joining two words but leaving out a letter or some letters.  Place an apostrophe ( ' ) where the letter or letters have been left out.**

Example:   did not  =  didn't

Write the contraction.

3.    a)   could not - _____

b)   he is - _____

c)   cannot - _____

## SENTENCE COMBINING:

4.  Ira will go to a museum tomorrow.
    He will go at 2:30 in the afternoon.

_____

_____

## CAPITALIZATION:

1. we left the last monday in june.

## PUNCTUATION:

**Do not place a comma between two items in a series.**

Example: They ate bacon and eggs.

**Place a comma after the first two items in a series if there are at least three items given.**

Example: Sue likes apples, pears, and bananas for lunch.

2. We saw bears monkeys and lions at the zoo

_____

## PARTS OF SPEECH:   ADJECTIVES

**An adjective is a describing word.**

Write the two adjectives that describe apples in this sentence.

3. I like red and juicy apples. _____ and _____

## SENTENCE COMBINING:

4. The gift has silver paper.
   It has a blue bow.

_____

_____

## CAPITALIZATION:

**Capitalize the name of a book if the title is only one word.**

Example:   the book, <u>Weasel</u>

1.  his mom read <u>bambi</u> to him.

## PUNCTUATION:

**If one person owns something, add '_s_.**

Example:  one hamster**'s** cage

2.  a car belonging to her dad = her _____ car

## PREFIXES/ROOTS/SUFFIXES:

**A root is any word without a part added at the beginning or at the end.**

Examples: smoothly    =    smooth **(root)**    +    ly  (suffix)

remake    =    re  (prefix)  +    make **(root)**

3.  The root of <u>jumping</u> is _____.

## SENTENCE COMBINING:

4.  His favorite food is steak.
    His favorite food is also cheese pizza.

    _____

    _____

## CAPITALIZATION:

**Capitalize the first word of a greeting of a letter.**
**Capitalize a person's name in the greeting of a letter.**

Examples:  **M**y dear friend,

**D**ear **S**usie,

1.  dear billy,

## PUNCTUATION:

**Place a comma after the greeting of a letter that you would write to a friend.**

Example:  Dear Stan,

2.  Dear Paul  _____

## PREFIXES/ROOTS/SUFFIXES:

**Some words are made by adding an ending called a suffix.**

Example:  fly   +   ing   =   flying
(root)      **(suffix)**

3.  ask  +  <u>ing</u>  =  _____

## SENTENCE COMBINING:

4.  Danny can't go.
Fran can go.

_____

_____

**DAY 54**

## CAPITALIZATION:

1.  dear ann,

    i miss you.

## PUNCTUATION:

2.  Tony are you sad

_____

## SYNONYMS/ANTONYMS/HOMONYMS:

**A synonym is a word that means the same or nearly the same as another word.**

Example:   little   -   tiny

3.  A synonym for <u>big</u> is _____.

## SENTENCE COMBINING:

4.  The deer heard a noise.
    The deer looked around.

_____

_____

_____

**CAPITALIZATION:**

1.  their wedding will be saturday, july 7.

**PUNCTUATION:**

2.  Linda shared candy nuts and chips

_____

**PREFIXES/ROOTS/SUFFIXES:**

**A prefix is placed in front of a root word.**
**A prefix has a meaning.**

Example:  **un** means <u>not</u>

un  +  happy    =    unhappy  (not happy)
**(prefix)**    (root)

3.  unsafe  =  un  +  safe

What does <u>unsafe</u> mean?  _____

**SENTENCE COMBINING:**

4.  Those chips are stale.
    This bread is stale, also.

_____

_____

_____

## CAPITALIZATION:

**Capitalize the name of a specific building or place.**

Examples:  **B**oston **A**rt **M**useum

**B**rushtown **F**ire **S**tation

1.  my friend and i went to the phoenix zoo*.

    *name of a specific zoo (place)

## PUNCTUATION:

**Place a hyphen ( - ) between two-word numbers between 21 and 99.**

Examples:  thirty-four        sixty-six

2.  Jills necklace has eighty two pearls

_____

## DICTIONARY:  ENTRIES

**Dictionary words are called entries. They are placed in alphabetical order.  The part of speech is placed after the word.**

| | | | | | |
|---|---|---|---|---|---|
| **n.** | **=** | **noun** | **adv.** | **=** | **adverb** |
| **pron.** | **=** | **pronoun** | **conj.** | **=** | **conjunction** |
| **v.** | **=** | **verb** | **intj.** | **=** | **interjection** |
| **adj.** | **=** | **adjective** | **prep.** | **=** | **preposition** |

flimsy, adj.  not sturdy

flute, n.  musical instrument

3.  What part of speech is <u>flimsy</u>? _____

## SENTENCE COMBINING:

4.  Tate wants to go to the library.
    Nobody can take him.

_____

_____

**CAPITALIZATION:**

1. their team practices at peoria sports complex*.

   *name of a specific building

**PUNCTUATION:**

**If one person or thing owns something, add 's.**

Examples: one girl**'s** bat
a pencil**'s** eraser

2. the dog has a dish = the _____ dish

**SUBJECT/VERB AGREEMENT:**

**Tense means time.  Present tense means time now.**

Example: A <u>girl</u> <u>swims</u> in a lake.

**If the subject is singular (one), add <u>s</u> to the verb.**

Example: One <u>boy</u> <u>bounces</u> a ball.

**If the subject is plural (more than one), do not add <u>s</u> to the verb.**
Example: Two <u>boys</u> <u>bounce</u> balls.

Write the verb that agrees with the subject.

3. That bell _____ (to sound) loud.

**SENTENCE COMBINING:**

4. Miss Smith smiled.
She handed me a paper.

_____

_____

## CAPITALIZATION:

1. have you been to firebird stadium*?

     *name of a specific place

## PUNCTUATION:

**If one person or thing owns something, add 's.**

> Example:   my friend**'s** mom

2. a cart has wheels  =  a _____ wheels

## SENTENCE TYPES:

**A statement tells something.**

> Example:   Nick plays the piano.

**A question asks something.**

> Example:   Is your room clean?

Name the sentence type.

3. The clerk dropped a dollar. _____

## SENTENCE COMBINING:

4. The coach handed Sue a trophy.
   The coach also handed Adam a trophy.

   _____

   _____

## CAPITALIZATION:

**Capitalize the first and last word of a title of a story, poem, or book.**

Example:   a nursery rhyme,  "**H**umpty **D**umpty"

1.  a book, <u>the farm</u>


## PUNCTUATION:

2.  No the bus wont stop here

_____


## PARTS OF SPEECH:   PRONOUNS

**Pronouns take the place of nouns.**
**Some pronouns are <u>I</u>, <u>he</u>, <u>she</u>, <u>we</u>, <u>they</u>, <u>you</u>, <u>who</u>, and <u>it</u>.**

Write a pronoun to replace the underlined noun in this sentence.

3.  <u>Boys</u> were playing tag in a yard.

_____ were playing tag in a yard.


## SENTENCE COMBINING:

4.  This floor is very shiny.
    This floor is very clean.

_____

_____

_____

## CAPITALIZATION:

**Capitalize the first and last word of a title of a story, poem, or book.**

Example:   a poem,  "The Seal"

1.   she likes the story, "sleeping beauty."

## PUNCTUATION:

**If a color and another describing word come in front of a word, do not place a comma between the color and the describing word.**

Example:   a big blue poster

2.   The red juicy apples werent in the basket

_____

## ALPHABETIZING:

Write these words in alphabetical order.

3.   flat        apple        card        fast        heart

a) _____      d) _____

b) _____      e) _____

c) _____

## SENTENCE COMBINING:

4.   Peter's cow won a ribbon at the fair.
     That happened yesterday.

_____

_____

**CAPITALIZATION:**

1. is mummy mountain in the state of arizona?

**PUNCTUATION:**

2. That large brown hen wont lay eggs

_____

**PARTS OF SPEECH:   ADVERBS**

**Some adverbs tell <u>how</u>.  They usually end in <u>ly</u>.**
**Adverbs that tells _how_ usually help to explain the verb.**

Example:   I <u>yelled</u> loudly.  (Loudly tells _how_ I yelled.)

Find the adverb that tells <u>how</u> Dr. Chan spoke:

3.   Dr. Chan spoke kindly to his patient.  _____

**SENTENCE COMBINING:**

4. Maria wrote a story.
   The story was about two monsters.

_____

_____

**CAPITALIZATION:**

1.  john and i went to broken arrow* to see our aunt.

    *name of a town

**PUNCTUATION:**

**If a number and another describing word come in front of a word, do not place a comma between the number and the describing word.**
                          Example:   my two front teeth

2.  Three black horses are in the field

_____

**PARTS OF SPEECH:   NOUNS**

**A noun names a person, place, or thing.**

Write two words that name <u>things</u> (nouns) in this sentence.

3.  Her brush is in the sink.   _____

                                _____

**SENTENCE COMBINING:**

4.  Forks are on the table.
    Knives and spoons are on the table.

_____

_____

**CAPITALIZATION:**

1. has micah gone to otter world*?

   *name of a (theme park) business

**PUNCTUATION:**

2. Dear Jay _____

**PARTS OF SPEECH:   CONJUNCTIONS**

   **Conjunctions join words or groups of words (phrases).
   The words <u>and</u>, <u>but</u>, and <u>or</u> are conjunctions.**

   Write a conjunction to join the following words.

3. a peanut butter _____ jelly sandwich

**SENTENCE COMBINING:**

4. Max loves shrimp salad.
   His sisters don't like shrimp salad.

   _____

   _____

   _____

**DAY 64**

## CAPITALIZATION:

1.  on memorial day,* we went to new york**.

         *name of a special day
         **name of a state

## PUNCTUATION:

**If one person or thing owns something, add 's to the word.**

2.  a house that a friend owns  =  a _____ house

## SUBJECTS:

**A subject tells <u>who</u> or <u>what</u> a sentence is about.**

Underline the subject.

3.  Two black cows ate in the barn.

## SENTENCE COMBINING:

4.  We cheered for my brother's team.
    The other team won.

    _____

    _____

    _____

## CAPITALIZATION:

**Capitalize only the first word in the closing of a letter.**

Examples:  **Y**our cousin,        **L**ove always,
           **T**oby               **G**randma

1.  your friend,

    carli

## PUNCTUATION:

2.  Wow  I ve nearly hit the target

_____

## PARTS OF SPEECH:   VERBS

**A verb tells <u>what is</u> or <u>what happens</u> (<u>does</u>) in a sentence.**

What word tells what the cows did?

3.  Two black cows ate in the barn.  _____

## SENTENCE COMBINING:

4.  They are drawing pictures.
    They are using chalk.

_____

_____

_____

**DAY 66**

**CAPITALIZATION:**

1.  see you soon,

    wendy

**PUNCTUATION:**

2.  a hat that Bill has  = _____ hat

**PARTS OF SPEECH:   VERBS**

> **Tense means time.**
> **Past tense means past time.  Something already happened.**
> **Most verbs add <u>ed</u> to form the past tense.**

>      Example:    Tony and Heidi <u>jumped</u> into a puddle.

> Write the past tense of this sentence.

3.  Yesterday, we _____ (to wash) our car.

**SENTENCE COMBINING:**

4.  Our friends are baking cookies.
    The cookies are for a bake sale.

    _____

    _____

    _____

## CAPITALIZATION:

**Capitalize abbreviations for states.**

Examples:   Colorado = **CO**         New York = **NY**

1.  cody's address is 15 bell street, reno, nv   89502.


## PUNCTUATION:

2.  a) a pet belonging to one girl  = one _____ pet

   b) the lid on a jar  = a _____ lid


## PARTS OF SPEECH:   INTERJECTIONS

**An interjection is a word or group of words (phrase) that shows excitement.  An exclamation mark ( ! ) is placed after an interjection.**

Example:   Hurrah!

Place an exclamation mark after each of the following interjections.

3.  a) Yeah          b) Wow


## SENTENCE COMBINING:

4.  I built a birdhouse.
   My mother helped me.

_____

_____

_____

**DAY 68**

## CAPITALIZATION:

1. is lake champlain in canada*?

   *name of a country

## PUNCTUATION:

**Underline the title of a book.**
**Place a short story in quotation marks (" ").**

   Examples:   a book, <u>The Yearling</u>     a short story, "Fire Bringer"

2. a) a book   -   Ira Sleeps Over

   b) a story   -   The Cat's Purr

## PARTS OF SPEECH:   CONJUNCTIONS

**A conjunction joins words or groups of words (phrases).**
**<u>And</u>, <u>but</u>, and <u>or</u> are conjunctions.**

   Write a conjunction to join the verbs in this sentence.

3. Laura sings _____ plays the flute every day.

## SENTENCE COMBINING:

4. Mark has a cat.
   The cat sleeps with Mark.

   _____

   _____

   _____

**CAPITALIZATION:**

1.  dear koko,

    i'll see you at your picnic.

              hugs and kisses,
              anna

**PUNCTUATION:**

**Underline the title of a book.**
**Place a short story in quotation marks (" ").**

    Examples:  a book, <u>The Duckling</u>      a short story, "The Snowman"

2.  a) a book   -   The Red Cloak

    b) a story   -   The Story of a Young Artist

**COMPOUND WORDS:**

**A compound word is made by joining two regular words.**

    Example:  ant  +  hill  =  anthill

3.  tooth  +  brush  =  _____

**SENTENCE COMBINING:**

4.  Ada plays school.
    Lexa plays school with her.

    _____

    _____

    _____

**DAY 70**

## CAPITALIZATION:

1.  we will fish in the salt river next friday, august 6.

## PUNCTUATION:

**Place a comma after the first two items if three items are in a series.**

Example:   Her sisters' names are Tina, Mary, and Jenny.

2.  Our flag is red white and blue

## SENTENCE TYPES:

**A statement tells something.  It ends with a period (.).**

Example:   Birds ate corn in the field.

**A question asks something.  It ends with a question mark (?).**

Example:   Have you taken your bath?

Name the sentence type.

3.  Their dad went shopping.  _____

## SENTENCE COMBINING:

4.  A plumber fixes sinks.
    A plumber fixes toilets, too.

_____

_____

_____

## CAPITALIZATION:

### Do not capitalize the seasons of the year.

Examples:    spring          autumn *or* fall
             summer          winter

1.  dear rick,

    in autumn, we will camp near skunk creek.

                        your friend,
                        maddy

## PUNCTUATION:

2.  Theyll be thirty years old on Jan 12 2020

## PARTS OF SPEECH:    PREPOSITIONS

**To, in, at, for, from, and of are common prepositions.
Each of these words may be followed by something you can
usually see (a noun or a pronoun).**

Examples:  **in**  =  in the *water*
           **at**  =  at *me*

Write a word or some words after each preposition.

3.      a) **for** _____

        b) **to** _____

## SENTENCE COMBINING:

4.  Jacy fell off a hay wagon.
    Jacy was not hurt.

    _____

    _____

**DAY 72**

## CAPITALIZATION:

1.  last year miss motts went to hawaii*.

    *name of a state

## PUNCTUATION:

**If one person or thing owns something, add 's.**
**If two or more persons or things own something—and that**
**word ends in s—add ' after the s.**

Examples:  one boy owns a bicycle  =  one boy's bicycle

two boys own the same bicycle  =  two boys' bicycle

2.  five pigs share (own) the same pen  = five _____ pen

## DICTIONARY:  SYLLABLES
**Words have different units of sound.**
**Some words say just one sound.  These are called**
**one-syllable words.  Some words have two units of sound.**

Examples:  run    (one syllable)
runner  =  run  ner    (two syllables)

Divide these words into syllables.

3.    a)  happy - _____    b)  mom - _____

## SENTENCE COMBINING:

4.  Mrs. Fay is going to the library.
Then, she is going to the store.

_____

_____

**CAPITALIZATION:**

**Capitalize the name of a language.**

Example:  **S**panish

1.  do you speak english?

**PUNCTUATION:**

**If two or more persons or things own something—and that word ends in s̲—add ' after the s̲.**

Example:  restroom used by all girls  =   girl**s'** restroom

2.  locker room for boys  =  _____ locker room

**DICTIONARY:   SYLLABLES**

**Words have different units of sound.**
**Some words say just one sound.  These are called one-syllable words.**
Example:   bear

Circle the one-syllable words.

3.  dog      ham       hammer       boat

**SENTENCE COMBINING:**

4.  Dave has gone to visit a sick friend.
    Jill has gone with him.

_____

_____

## CAPITALIZATION:

**Capitalize the first word when someone has spoken.
This is called a direct quotation.**

Example:   Bibi said, "**M**y dog had two puppies."

1.   miss bota asked, "what is your name?"

## PUNCTUATION:

**Place what someone says in quotation marks (" ").**

Example:   Ryan asked, "Where's your house?"

2.  A small child cried,  Where is my momma

_____

## PARTS OF SPEECH:   ADVERBS

**Some adverbs tell <u>how</u>.  They usually end in <u>ly</u>.
Adverbs that tell *how* usually help to explain the verb.**

Find the adverb that tells <u>how</u> she touched the bowl.

3.    She touched the glass bowl gently.   _____

## SENTENCE COMBINING:

4.  The cake is chocolate.
The cake has white frosting with pink sprinkles.

_____

_____

## CAPITALIZATION:

**Capitalize the first word when someone has spoken.
This is called a direct quotation.**

Example:   Paco asked, "Is lunch ready?"

1.   mark asked, "how are you?"

## PUNCTUATION:

**Place what someone says in quotation marks (" ").**

Example:   The teacher said, "Please pass your papers."

2.   Nick said,  Our car has a flat tire.

---

## DICTIONARY:   GUIDE WORDS

**At the top of every dictionary page are two words.  These are called
guide words.  The first word is the first word on that page.  The
word across from it is the last word on that page.**

Example:   **rain            red**

Rain is the first word on the page.  Red is the last word on the page.
Do you see that *rod* will not be on that page? *R-o-d* comes after *r-e-d*.

3.   Will ram be found on a page with guide words rain and red? _____

## SENTENCE COMBINING:

4.   Joy likes carrots.
     She also likes corn and green beans.

---

---

**DAY 76**

## CAPITALIZATION:

1. the people of france* speak the french language.
   *name of a country

## PUNCTUATION:

2. Theyre reading Bubble Bubble*
   *name of a book

_____

## SYNONYMS/ANTONYMS/HOMONYMS:

### Antonyms are words with opposite meanings.

Example:   hot  -  cold

3. Write an antonym for <u>good</u>. _____

## SENTENCE COMBINING:

4. Tate and I have snowball fights in the winter.
   Tate and I sled in the winter.

_____

_____

_____

**CAPITALIZATION:**

1.  we visited her at dover general hospital.

**PUNCTUATION:**

**Place a comma after a person spoken to.**

Examples:  Patty, let's go!        Let's go, Patty!

2.  Miss Jones may we read

_____

**PARTS OF SPEECH:    ADJECTIVES**

**Adjectives can be describing words.**    Example: **cute** baby

**Adjectives can tell which one(s).**    Example: **this** bug

**Adjectives can tell how many.**    Example: **five** parrots
                                                                **some** people

Choose the two adjectives that tell <u>how many</u> in the following sentence.

3.  Four classes sang many songs.    _____    _____

**SENTENCE COMBINING:**

4.  They have to clean their room.
    It is a mess.

_____

_____

_____

**DAY 78**

## CAPITALIZATION:

**Capitalize the name of a club or an organization.**

Example:   **W**elcome **W**agon **C**lub

1.   her brother belongs to the rangers club.

## PUNCTUATION:

**Place a comma after <u>Yes</u> or <u>No</u> at the beginning of a sentence.**

Examples:   Yes, we like it.          No, we can't play now.

2.   Yes Im going with you

_____


## PARTS OF SPEECH:   PRONOUNS

**Pronouns take the place of nouns.**

Example:   Tom and Jerry   **=   they**

Write the pronoun for the underlined word in the following sentence.

3.   <u>Mandy</u> is in the army.

_____ is in the army.


## SENTENCE COMBINING:

4.   Cereal is a breakfast food.
     Pancakes and eggs are breakfast foods.

_____

_____

_____

## CAPITALIZATION:

1.  has mr. james joined young life*?

    *name of an organization

## PUNCTUATION:

2.  The lambs wool is white and fluffy

_____

## PARTS OF SPEECH:   ADVERBS

**Adverbs can tell <u>how</u> and <u>when</u>.**

**Adverbs can also tell <u>where</u>.**

Example:   I want to stay <u>here</u>.

Write the adverb that tells <u>where</u> Pat has gone.

3.  Has Pat gone there?   _____

## SENTENCE COMBINING:

4.  Jana swims.
    Jana skis.
    Jana takes dance lessons.

_____

_____

_____

**DAY 80**

## CAPITALIZATION:

1. pott's grocery store is in virginia*.
   *name of a state

## PUNCTUATION:

2. Nov 30 2015 _____

## PREFIXES/ROOTS/SUFFIXES:

**Some words are made by adding an ending called a suffix.**

Example: play + **s** = play**s**
(root)     (suffix)

**Some words are made by adding a prefix before the main (root) word.**

Example: **re** + play = **re**play
(prefix)   (root)

**Some words have a prefix, a root, and a suffix.**

<u>sub</u>          +          <u>marine</u>          +          <u>s</u>
(a **prefix** that          (a **root** word that          (a **suffix** that can
means *under*)          means *water*)          mean *more than one*)

3. a) sub + marine + s = _____

   b) Knowing word parts can help you figure out the meaning of a word.
      Do you know what a submarine is?  A submarine is

      _____.


## SENTENCE COMBINING:

4. This cup is chipped.
   Leah cut her lip on it.


   _____


   _____

## CAPITALIZATION:

1.  my mom belongs to the friendship club.

## PUNCTUATION:

2.  Friday December 5 2020

---

## DICTIONARY:   ENTRIES

**Dictionary words are called entries. They are placed in alphabetical order.  The part of speech is placed after the word.**

<u>**The abbreviations may be slightly different in some dictionaries.**</u>
Examples:   pronoun = *pro.*         verb = *vt.* or *vi.*

| | | | | | |
|---|---|---|---|---|---|
| **n.** | **=** | **noun** | **adv.** | **=** | **adverb** |
| **pron.** | **=** | **pronoun** | **conj.** | **=** | **conjunction** |
| **v.** | **=** | **verb** | **intj.** | **=** | **interjection** |
| **adj.** | **=** | **adjective** | **prep.** | **=** | **preposition** |

lad, n.  a little boy

pretty, adj.  nice to look at

Look at the part of speech for this dictionary entry:

grassy, adj.  covered with grass

3.   What does **adj.** mean?  _____

## SENTENCE COMBINING:

4.  The clerk smiled.
    He gave me change.

---

---

## CAPITALIZATION:

1. the brooklyn bridge is in new york.

## PUNCTUATION:

**Place a comma between a city and a state.**

**Do not place a comma between a state and a zip code.**

Example:   Orem, Utah   84058

2.  La Quinta  CA   92253   _____
      (city)        (state) (zip code)

## SUBJECTS/VERBS:

**The subject is <u>who</u> or <u>what</u> the sentence is about.**

**The verb is what <u>is</u> (<u>was</u>) or what <u>happens</u> (<u>happened</u>).**
**If the event already happened, the verb will usually end in <u>ed</u>.**

**Example:**   The <u>man</u> <u>chopped</u> wood.

Underline the subject once and the verb twice.

3.   An artist painted a picture.

## SENTENCE COMBINING:

4.  My grandpa walks every day.
    He walks two miles.

_____

_____

## CAPITALIZATION:

1. the girls met last thursday at keys elementary school.

## PUNCTUATION:

**Underline the title of a book.**

Example:   The Kids' Cookbook

**Place a short story in quotation marks (" ").**

Example:  "The Ice-Cube Club"

Punctuate these titles.

2.  a) a book, The Rainbow Fish          b) a short story, Driving on Ice

## PARTS OF SPEECH:   VERBS

**A contraction is made up of two words.**
**A contraction has a letter or some letters left out.**
**Those letters are replaced by an apostrophe ( ' ).**

Example:   do not  =  don't

3.     The contraction for <u>does not</u> is _____.

## SENTENCE COMBINING:

4. Jason grinned.
Jason hid his hands behind his back.

_____

_____

**DAY 84**

## CAPITALIZATION:

**Capitalize the names of islands and other land forms.**

Examples:   Canary Islands
                    Cape of Good Hope

1.   his dad and he went to treasure island.

## PUNCTUATION:

**Do not use a period after state postal codes.**

Examples:   Iowa  =  **IA**
                    Utah  =  **UT**

2.   Write your state's postal code.  _____

## PARTS OF SPEECH:   VERBS

**A contraction has an apostrophe ( ' ) where a letter or some letters have been left out.**

3.   a)  would not - _____      c)  here is -  _____

      b)  I have - _____      d)  you will -  _____

## SENTENCE COMBINING:

4.   Tommy runs faster than Bart.
      Tommy runs faster than Jenny.

      _____

      _____

      _____

**CAPITALIZATION:**

1.  on presidents' day*, they went to the colorado river.

    *name of a special day

**PUNCTUATION:**

**If one person or thing owns something, add 's.
If two or more persons or things own something—and that
word ends in s—add ' after the s.**

Examples:   a camper's tent

two campers' tent

2.  a) a surfboard of one girl = one _____ surfboard

b) a surfboard owned by two girls = two _____ surfboard

**PARTS OF SPEECH:   VERBS**

Write the contractions.

3.   a)  I am - _____        c)  who is - _____

b)  are not - _____        d)  they are - _____

**SENTENCE COMBINING:**

4.  Jacy is making a bracelet.
The bracelet is black.
The bracelet is for his brother.

_____

_____

_____

**DAY 86**

## CAPITALIZATION:

1.  rusty's dad owns a restaurant called sky diner.

## PUNCTUATION:

2.  a)  a laptop owned by one nurse = one _____ laptop

    b)  a workshop for many nurses = _____ workshop

## PARTS OF SPEECH:   SENTENCE TYPES

**A statement tells something.  It ends with a period ( . ).**
Example:   These peas are cold.

**A question asks something.  It ends with a question mark ( ? ).**
Example:   Do you like peas?

**A command tells you to do something.  It ends with a period ( . ).**
Example:   Pass the peas, please.

Name the type of sentence.

3.    a)  I need a paper clip. _____

      b)  Put these away. _____

## SENTENCE COMBINING:

4.  The streetlights have come on.
    It is dark.

    _____

    _____

    _____

## CAPITALIZATION:

1. did mrs. a. vargas come?

## PUNCTUATION:

2. Little Rock  AR    72201    _____
    (city)      (state)  (zip code)

## PARTS OF SPEECH:   PRONOUNS

**Pronouns take the place of nouns.**

        Example:   Vicky pitched a <u>ball</u> fast.
                       Vicky pitched **<u>it</u>** fast.

Write your name in the blank in the first sentence.  Use a pronoun to replace your name in the second sentence.

3.    a) _____ wants a drink.

      b) _____ want a drink.

## SENTENCE COMBINING:

4.  I am going to the beach.
    I am taking a raft.

_____

_____

_____

## CAPITALIZATION:

**Capitalize the name of a specific building or place.**

Example:   **R**osson **H**ouse **M**useum

1.   is hope church on daisy drive?

## PUNCTUATION:

**If an address appears in a sentence, place a comma between the street address and the town (city).  Place a comma between the town (city) and the state.  Do not place a comma between the state and the zip code.**

Example:   Go to 2 W. Adams Street, Ruidoso, New Mexico   88346.

2.   He lives at 102 S Mill Lane Lubbock TX  79493

_____

## PARTS OF SPEECH:   INTERJECTIONS

**An interjection is a word or phrase (group of words) that shows excitement.  An exclamation mark ( ! ) is placed after an interjection.**

Example:   Yippee!

3.  Write an interjection on this line.  _____

## SENTENCE COMBINING:

4.  They are cutting out stars.
They are cutting out flowers.
The stars and flowers are for their scrapbook.

_____

_____

_____

## CAPITALIZATION:

1.  may we go to parks mall* today?

    *name of a business

## PUNCTUATION:

2.  a) nuts belonging to one squirrel = _____ nuts

    b) nuts belonging to many squirrels = _____ nuts

## PARTS OF SPEECH:   VERBS

**Tense means time.**
**Present tense means now.**
        Example:   Joy <u>laughs</u> loudly.

**Past tense means something has already happened.**
        Example:   Joy <u>laughed</u> loudly.

Write the correct verb in the blank.

3.  a)  Right now, Dad _____ (to cook) dinner.

    b)  Yesterday, Dad _____ (to cook) dinner.

## SENTENCE COMBINING:

4.  We went ice skating.
    We went to a pond.
    We had fun.

    _____

    _____

    _____

**CAPITALIZATION:**

1.  a storm hit the bahama islands in september.

**PUNCTUATION:**

> **Place a comma at the end of a greeting and a closing of a letter that you would write to a friend.**
> Examples:     Dear Joy,   (greeting)
>                        Your friend,   (closing)

2.  Dear Tim             _____

    Youre a good friend     _____

         Your pal          _____

         Ron

**PARTS OF SPEECH:   PRONOUNS**

> **Pronouns take the place of nouns.**
> Example:     Sit beside <u>Stan</u>.
>                    Sit beside **him**.
>
> Write your name in the blank in the first sentence.  Use a pronoun to replace your name in the second sentence.

3.  a) Come with _____.
    b) Come with _____.

**SENTENCE COMBINING:**

4.  Fran opened the door.
    Her puppy ran out.

    _____

    _____

**CAPITALIZATION:**
   **Capitalize the first and last word of a title of a story, a poem, or a book.**
   Example:   a book, "**W**ild **W**eather"

1.  a story, "upside down"

**PUNCTUATION:**
   **Use a colon with time.**     Example:   5**:**30

2.  His sister will marry at 2 00 in Lutz Florida

_____

**PARTS OF SPEECH:   PRONOUNS**
   **Pronouns take the place of nouns.**
   **Some pronouns show ownership: <u>my</u>, <u>his</u>, <u>her</u>, <u>our</u>, <u>their</u>, <u>your</u>, <u>whose</u>, and <u>its</u>.**
                                               *his*
            Example:   Peter forgot Peter's jacket.

   Write your name in the first 2 blanks.  Write a pronoun to replace your name in the second sentence.

3.  _____ likes _____ friends.

      I like _____ friends.

**SYNONYNMS/ANTONYMS/HOMONYMS:**
   **Synonyms are words that mean nearly the same.**
                  Example:   pull  -  tug

4.  A synonym for <u>angry</u> is _____.

**SENTENCE COMBINING:**

5.  Jana likes to hike.
   Her brother likes to hike, too.

_____

_____

**DAY 92**

## CAPITALIZATION:

1. is oakwood college on dale street?

## PUNCTUATION:

**Place an apostrophe ( ' ) where a letter or letters have been left out.**

Examples:  what is  = what's          of the clock  =  o'clock

2. He knows that youre here _____

## PARTS OF SPEECH:   PRONOUNS

**Pronouns take the place of nouns.**
Example:    Some <u>birds</u> flew away.
<u>They</u> flew away.

Write a pronoun for the underlined words.

3.  a) Buy cards for <u>Jina</u> and her <u>mother</u>.

b) Buy cards for _____.

## SENTENCE TYPES:

**A question asks something.  It ends with a question mark ( ? ).**
Example:   Do you like peas**?**

**A command tells you to do something.  It ends with a period ( . ).**
Example:   Pass the peas, please**.**

Name the type of sentence.

4.   Put these away. _____

## SENTENCE COMBINING:

5.  Matt plays soccer.
His sister plays soccer, also.

_____

_____

**CAPITALIZATION:**

1.  has aunt kate read the book, <u>jacob's ladder</u>?

**PUNCTUATION:**

2.  The party will start at 6 30 on Saturday July 13

_____

**PARTS OF SPEECH:    NOUNS**

> **Plural means more than one.  Most words add <u>s</u> to form the plural.  Words ending in <u>sh</u>, <u>ch</u>, <u>s</u>, <u>x</u>, and <u>z</u> add <u>es</u>.**

> Write the plural of each noun.

3.  a)  peach - _____    c)  slush - _____

> b)  pear - _____    d)  box - _____

**SYNONYMS/ANTONYMS/HOMONYMS:**

4.  A synonym for <u>speedy</u> is _____.

**SENTENCE COMBINING:**

5.  The ball is red.
    It has a wide blue stripe.
    It belongs to Tara.

_____

_____

**DAY 94**

## CAPITALIZATION:

1. did grandma liss read you the book, <u>the rainbow fish</u>?

## PUNCTUATION:

2. Jills scooter is yellow and black _____

## PARTS OF SPEECH:   ADVERBS

**Some adverbs tell <u>how</u>.  Adverbs that tell *how* usually help to explain the verb. They usually end in <u>ly</u>.  However, some do not.**

Example:   She threw the ball **hard**.

Find the adverb that tells <u>how</u> the teacher runs.

3.   That teacher runs fast.   _____

## ALPHABETIZING:

Write these words in alphabetical order.

4. deer      banana      elk      lamb

a) _____     c) _____

b) _____     d) _____

## SENTENCE COMBINING:

5. Kim is washing his truck.
   He is waxing it, too.

_____

_____

## CAPITALIZATION:

**Capitalize the name of a language.**

Example:  **G**erman

1.  we learned to speak english at age five.

## PUNCTUATION:

**Place what someone says in quotation marks (" ").**

2.  Dora asked,  Will you hold this?

_____

## PARTS OF SPEECH:   ADJECTIVES
**Some adjectives describe.**     Example:   **sleek**, **new** boat

Find two adjectives that describe in the following sentence.

3.   A furry kitten slept on a soft blanket.     _____ kitten
                                                 _____ blanket

## PARTS OF SPEECH:   PRONOUNS

**Pronouns take the place of nouns.  Some pronouns show ownership:  <u>my</u>, <u>his</u>, <u>her</u>, <u>our</u>, <u>their</u>, <u>your</u>, <u>whose</u>, and <u>its</u>.**

*her*
Example:    Jana lost Jana's jacket.

Write a possessive pronoun to replace the underlined word:

4.  <u>Jay</u> likes _____ turtle.

## SENTENCE COMBINING:

5.  Carli is making dinner.
    Carli is making meat loaf.
    She is also making mashed potatoes and peas.

_____

_____

**DAY 96**

**CAPITALIZATION:**

1.  last winter, captain bree was sent to scotland*.

    *name of a country

**PUNCTUATION:**

2.  Have you ever been to Buffalo New York

_____

**PARTS OF SPEECH:    ADVERBS**
   **Do not use <u>not</u> and <u>nothing</u> in the same sentence.**

   Write the correct word.

3.    We are not searching for _____ ( nothing, anything ).

**PARTS OF SPEECH:   VERBS**

   **Tense means time.  Past tense means past time.  Something already happened.  Most verbs add <u>ed</u> to make the past tense.**

   Write the past tense.

4.  Yesterday, they _____ (to look) for a pet snake.

**SENTENCE COMBINING:**

5.  Kala ate eggs for breakfast.
    She also ate toast.
    She also ate ham.

_____

_____

_____

## CAPITALIZATION:

**Capitalize the name of a school, college, or any place of learning.**

Example:   Little **Bo Peep Preschool**

1.  during spring break, our family went to naco school in mexico*.
       *name of a country

## PUNCTUATION:

2.  They met on Friday March 31 2006

_____

## PARTS OF SPEECH:   ADJECTIVES

**Adjectives can be describing words that tell <u>what kind</u>.**

Write an adjective that tells <u>what kind</u>.

3.  a) _____ dog      b) _____ house

## PARTS OF SPEECH:   NOUNS

Write the plural of each noun.

4.  a) stick - _____      b) ranch - _____

## SENTENCE COMBINING:

5.  Todd picked up a stone.
    He threw it into the creek.

_____

_____

**DAY 98**

**CAPITALIZATION:**

1.  they went to ellis park on labor day*.

     *name of a special day

**PUNCTUATION:**

**If one person or thing owns something, add 's.
If two or more persons or things own something—and that
word ends in s—add ' after the s.**

Examples:  my aunt's keys          my two aunts' apartment

2.  a) a hotel room for my uncle = _____ hotel room

     b) a hotel room for my two uncles = _____ hotel room

**PARTS OF SPEECH:   VERBS**
Write the contraction.

3.   a)  cannot - _____          c)  I shall - _____

      b)  where is - _____         d)  was not - _____

**SUBJECTS/VERBS:**

**The subject tells <u>who</u> or <u>what</u> the sentence is about.  Place one
line under the subject.**

**The verb tells what <u>is</u> or what <u>happens</u>.  Place two lines under the verb.**

Example:   <u>Lions</u> <u>roar</u>.

Place one line under the subject and two lines under the verb.

4.  Birds fly.

**SENTENCE COMBINING:**

5.  Do you want a glass of milk for a snack?
    Do you want a banana, too?

    _____

    _____

    _____

## CAPITALIZATION:

1.  did aunt koko come to the united states to attend gateway college?

## PUNCTUATION:

**Place what someone says in quotation marks (" ").**

2.  Josh asked,  Did Mom run errands today

_____

## PARTS OF SPEECH:    ADVERBS
**Do not use <u>not</u> (<u>n't</u>) and <u>nothing</u> in the same sentence.**

Write the correct word:

3.  They wouldn't eat _____ ( nothing, anything ).

## SUBJECT/VERB AGREEMENT:

**Tense means time.  Present tense means at this time or now.**

Write the present tense of this sentence.

4.  John _____ (to like) beef bacon.

## SENTENCE COMBINING:

5.  The man waved.
    The man stood up.

_____

_____

_____

**DAY 100**

## CAPITALIZATION:

1.  are uncle tom and i invited next christmas?


## PUNCTUATION:
**If a color and another describing word come in front of a word, do not place a comma between the color and the describing word.**

> Example:   a little black bunny

2.  Havent you eaten tiny green peas

_____


## PARTS OF SPEECH:   ADVERBS

**Some adverbs tell <u>when</u>.  Adverbs that tell *when* usually help to explain the verb.**

> Example:    I want to leave **now**.

Find the adverb that tells <u>when</u> the dancers will eat.

3.   The dancers will eat lunch later.   _____

## PARTS OF SPEECH:   VERBS

**Some verbs show action.**
What verb tells what we did yesterday?

4.   We skated yesterday.   _____


## SENTENCE COMBINING:

5.  Paco bought a bowling ball.
It is for his sister.

_____

_____

## CAPITALIZATION:

1.  the red hat society* will meet next thursday.
    *name of a club

## PUNCTUATION:

2.  Wow  Both of my sisters artwork won blue ribbons

_____

## PARTS OF SPEECH:   NOUNS

**Nouns name a person, place, or thing.**

Find a noun that names a <u>person</u> and a noun that names a <u>place</u>.

3.  Her dad went to a rodeo.  a) person - _____    b) place - _____

## PARTS OF SPEECH:   VERBS

**Present tense means time now.**
**Past tense means something already happened.**

4.  a)  I _____ (to want) an apple now.

    b)  Yesterday, I _____ (to want) yogurt.

## SENTENCE COMBINING:

5.  Their gate is made of iron.
    It is black.
    It is heavy.

_____

_____

**DAY 102**

**CAPITALIZATION:**

1. pam and i went to the smokey mountains in tennessee*.

   *name of a state

**PUNCTUATION:**

**Place a comma after <u>Yes</u> or <u>No</u> at the beginning of a sentence.**

Example:   Yes, we are sure.

2. No our dog doesnt bite

_____

**PARTS OF SPEECH:   VERBS**

**Future tense refers to something that <u>will be</u> or <u>will happen</u>.**
Examples:   I <u>shall go</u>.
You <u>will stay</u>.

3. The train _____ (to stop) here.

**COMPOUND WORDS:**

**A compound word is made by joining two regular words.**

Example:   board  +  walk  =  boardwalk

4. hall  +  way  =  _____

**SENTENCE COMBINING:**

5. Katy's mom has a truck.
   The truck is yellow.
   It has blue stripes.

_____

**CAPITALIZATION:**

1.  dear mike,

      i like you.

         your friend,

         bo

**PUNCTUATION:**
  **Underline the title of a book:**     Country Fair
  **Place a short story in quotation marks (" "):**    "My Good Day"

2.  a)  a short story, When the Clock Was Sick

    b)  a book, If I Had a Gorilla

**SYNONYMS/ANTONYMS/HOMONYMS:**

3.  A synonym for glad is _____.

**SUBJECT/VERB AGREEMENT:**
  **Tense means time.  Present tense means time now.**
  **If the subject is singular (one), add an s to the verb.**

      Example:   One friend golfs.

  **If the subject is plural (more than one), do not add an s to the verb.**
      Example:   Two friends golf.

4.  This paper _____ (to rip) easily.

**SENTENCE COMBINING:**

5.  Dark clouds rolled in.
    It began to rain.

    _____

    _____

**DAY 104**

## CAPITALIZATION:

**Capitalize the name of a body of water: ocean, sea, lake, or river.**

1. is lake pleasant near the pacific ocean?


## PUNCTUATION:

Punctuate the greeting and closing of this friendly letter.

2. Dear Fred _____
    Let's go to the park.
        Your friend _____
        Toni


## PARTS OF SPEECH:    ADVERBS
**Do not use <u>not</u> (<u>n't</u>) and <u>nothing</u> in the same sentence.**

Write the correct word:

3. We don't have _____ ( nothing, anything ) for a snack.


## SUBJECT/VERB AGREEMENT:
**Tense means time.  Present tense means time now.**
**I f the subject is singular (one), add an <u>s</u> to the verb.**

Example:  A <u>dog</u> <u>barks</u>.

**If the subject is plural (more than one), do not add an <u>s</u> to the verb.**
Example:  <u>Dogs</u> <u>bark</u>.

4. His poodle _____ (to stand) on his hind legs.


## SENTENCE COMBINING:

5. This pillow is made of velvet.
    It has tiny purple buttons.

    _____

    _____

## CAPITALIZATION:

1.  his sister went to oak mountain state park near pelham, alabama.

## PUNCTUATION:

2.  Yuck  Their dog has fleas _____

## PARTS OF SPEECH:   ADJECTIVES

**Adjectives can be describing words.**   Example: **fun** game

**Adjectives can tell which one(s).**   Example: **those** forks

**Adjectives can tell how many.**   Example: **six** eggs
   **many** hives

Choose the two adjectives that tell <u>which one(s)</u>.

3.  Put these cups in that box.   _____   _____

## ALPHABETIZING:

Write these words in alphabetical order.

4.  tale   ship   open   mole

a) _____   c) _____

b) _____   d) _____

## SENTENCE COMBINING:

5.  An emu is a bird.
    It lays eggs.
    It cannot fly.

_____

_____

**CAPITALIZATION:**

1.  their family moved to coe street in november.

**PUNCTUATION:**
> **Place a comma after a person to whom you are speaking.  If the name ends a sentence, place a comma after the word that appears before the name.**
>> Examples:  Kim, stop that.        Stop that, Kim.

2.  Miss Carr may we pass out papers

_____

**PARTS OF SPEECH:   PREPOSITIONS**
> **At, in, for, from, of, and to are common prepositions. They may be followed by something you can see (a noun or a pronoun).**
>> Examples:  for **you** (pronoun)        at the **pool** (noun)

> Write a word or some words after each preposition.

3.   a) **in** _____

   b) **from** _____

**DICTIONARY:   SYLLABLES**

> **Some words say just one sound and are one-syllable words: bug.**

> Circle any one-syllable words.

4.  fan        pepper        crayon        share        drill

**SENTENCE COMBINING:**

5.  This milk is sour.
    This milk tastes bad.

_____

_____

**CAPITALIZATION:**

1.  in january, her uncle is moving to italy*.

    *name of a country

**PUNCTUATION:**
**If two or more persons or things own something—and that word ends in s—add ' after the s.**

> Example:  a closet shared by two girls   =   girls' closet

2.  blocks used by many toddlers  = _____ blocks

**SYNONYNMS/ANTONYMS/HOMONYMS:**

**Antonyms are words with opposite meanings.**

> Example:   few  -  many

3.  Write an antonym for back. _____

**SUBJECTS/VERBS:**

**The subject is who or what the sentence is about.**
**The verb is what is (was) or what happens (happened).**

> Example:   A bus stops here.

Underline the subject once and the verb twice.

4.  Cows eat grass.

**SENTENCE COMBINING:**

5.  Beavers do not live in Florida.
    Beavers do not live in Mexico.

_____

_____

**DAY 108**

**CAPITALIZATION:**

1.  dr. and mrs. cobb want to go to yellowstone national park.

**PUNCTUATION:**

**Place a comma between a city and state.**

**Do not place a comma between a state and a zip code.**

Example:   Orem, Utah   84058

2.  Mrs Diaz lives at 22 East Woods Dr Saline MI   48176

_____

**PARTS OF SPEECH:   PREPOSITIONS**

**At, in, for, from, of, and to are common prepositions.**

Write a word or some words after each preposition.

3.   a) **of** _____

b) **at** _____

**RHYMING WORDS:**

4.  A word that rhymes with flame is _____.

**SENTENCE COMBINING:**

5.  Molly likes to ski.
She does not like to skate.

_____

_____

## CAPITALIZATION:

**Capitalize the name of a specific place.**

Examples:  **L**ory **S**tate **P**ark

**O**ld **G**ranbury **T**own **S**quare

1.  has dr. jacobs been to brookside gardens* in wheaton, maryland?

    *name of a specific place

## PUNCTUATION:

2.  No I dont want pie cake or pudding

_____

## ALPHABETIZING:

Write these words in alphabetical order.

3.  grape      ink      king      harp

a)  _____          c)  _____

b)  _____          d)  _____

## PREFIXES/ROOTS/SUFFIXES:

**A root is any word without an important part added at the beginning or a part added at the end.**

Examples:  remove      =      re      +      **move**
              dances      =      **dance**      +      s

4.  The root of <u>remakes</u> is _____.

## SENTENCE COMBINING:

5.  My friend laughed.
    Tears rolled down her cheeks.

_____

_____

**CAPITALIZATION:**

1. our aunt jo works at moss school.

**PUNCTUATION:**

**Place what someone says in quotation marks (" ").**

Example: "Come here!" yelled Lee.

2. Are you ready  asked Ann

_____

**PARTS OF SPEECH:   ADVERBS**

**Some adverbs tell <u>when</u> and help to explain the verb.**

Example:   You are **always** on time.

Find the adverb that tells <u>when</u> the show will start.

3.   Our show will start soon.   _____

**SUBJECT/VERB:**

Underline the subject once and the verb twice.

4. Bats fly at night.

**SENTENCE COMBINING:**

5. A raccoon has a chunky body.
   A raccoon has a broad head.
   A raccoon has a bushy tail.

_____

_____

## CAPITALIZATION:

1. our class drew pictures on columbus day*.
    *name of a special day

## PUNCTUATION:

**Remember:  Do not use a period after state postal codes.**

Examples:   Vermont = **VT**          Georgia = **GA**

2.   Punctuate this address of an envelope.

Beth R Parker          _____
12 N Ash Street        _____
Moore OK   73160       _____

## PARTS OF SPEECH:   VERBS

Write the contractions.

3.   a)  you are - _____        c)  is not - _____

     b)  do not - _____         d)  they will - _____

## PREFIXES/ROOTS/SUFFIXES:

**Some words are made by adding a prefix before the main word (root).**

Example:   un + do = undo

4.   What word is made by adding <u>non</u>, a prefix, to the root, <u>stop</u>? _____

## SENTENCE COMBINING:

5.   Alligators live in China.
     The only other country where alligators live is the United States.

    _____

    _____

## CAPITALIZATION:

1.  have you seen a picture of london bridge?

## PUNCTUATION:

2.  She was given a grey coat a black cape and a white hat

---

## DICTIONARY:    GUIDE WORDS

**Two guide words are listed at the top of each dictionary page.
The first word tells you the first word listed on that page.
The word beside it tells you the last word listed on that page.**

Example:    gate            gum

3.  Will the word <u>glue</u> be found on a dictionary page with the guide words, <u>gate</u> and <u>gum</u>?  _____

## DIFFICULT WORDS:

<u>Their</u> is a possessive pronoun:    They pulled **their** sled.
<u>There</u> is an adverb telling *where*:    Jacob wants to go **there**.
<u>They're</u> is a contraction for *they are*:    I know that **they're** finished.

Circle the correct word:

4.  ( There, Their, They're ) playing two-square.

## SENTENCE COMBINING:

5.  Micah wants to ski soon.
Jenny and Peter want to ski soon, too.

_____

_____

## CAPITALIZATION:

**Capitalize the first word, the last word, and all important words in a title.  Do not capitalize <u>a</u>, <u>an</u>, <u>the</u>, <u>and</u>, <u>but</u>, <u>or</u>, <u>nor</u>, and prepositions of four or less letters (<u>of</u>, <u>to</u>, <u>for</u>, <u>from</u>, and <u>in</u>) within a title.**

        Examples:   <u>L</u>ucy <u>G</u>oose <u>G</u>oes to <u>T</u>exas

                  "<u>F</u>riends and <u>A</u>nimals"

1.  a)  <u>the golden egg</u>

     b)  "gulp the lion"

## PUNCTUATION:

2.  Sam will you read me the book named Professor Wormbug

_____

## PARTS OF SPEECH:   ADJECTIVES

**Some adjectives tell <u>how many</u>.**

       Example:   **Some** butterflies have **no** bright colors.

     Write the adjectives that tell <u>how many</u>:

3.   Several kittens slept on one big pillow.   _____ kittens

                                              _____ pillow

## DIFFICULT WORDS:
     Circle the correct word:

4.  a) ( It's, Its ) the truth.      b) ( Their, They're, There ) cat had kittens.

## SENTENCE COMBINING:

5.  Kirk broke eggs into a bowl.
     Marco beat the eggs.

_____

_____

**DAY 114**

## CAPITALIZATION:

1.  they are fans of the phoenix suns*.
    *name of a basketball team

## PUNCTUATION:

Punctuate this address:

2.  Mr Fred Smith            _____

    12 Green Apple Ave       _____

    Dallas Texas   75214     _____

## PARTS OF SPEECH:   NOUNS

**Nouns name persons, places, and things.**

Circle any nouns that name <u>things</u> in this sentence:

3.  The old coin is on the table.

## PARTS OF SPEECH:   CONJUNCTIONS

**Conjunctions are connecting words.  <u>And</u>, <u>but</u>, and <u>or</u> are three conjunctions.**

Use the conjunction that makes sense.

4.  Maddy wants soup, a sandwich, _____ a salad for lunch.

## SENTENCE COMBINING:

5.  Carla bought a box.
    The box is made of glass.
    The box plays music.

    _____

    _____

**CAPITALIZATION:**

1. i want to go to bear island in lake superior.

**PUNCTUATION:**

2. Jimmys cousin didnt take his picture

---

**PARTS OF SPEECH:   ADJECTIVES**

> **Adjectives are describing words.**

> Write the two adjectives.

3. Brown bugs crawled in the tall grass.      _____ bugs
_____ grass

**PARTS OF SPEECH:   VERBS**

> **Verbs often show action.**

> Write **A** on the line if the verb shows action.

4. a) _____ jump          Mary <u>jumped</u> over a bench.

   b) _____ chase         Our cat <u>chases</u> our dog.

   c) _____ seem          You <u>seem</u> happy.

**SENTENCE COMBINING:**

5. Egg Lake is in Canada.
   Goose Lake is close to Egg Lake.

   _____

   _____

   _____

**DAY 116**

## CAPITALIZATION:

1. my aunt belongs to star dance club.

## PUNCTUATION:

2. a) a cage belonging to one gerbil = one _____ cage

   b) a cage belonging to many gerbils = _____ cage

## SENTENCE TYPES

**A statement tells something. It ends with a period ( . ).** You are nice.
**A question asks something. It ends with a question mark ( ? ).** May I?
**A command tells you to do something. It ends with a period ( . ).** Sit.
   Name the type of sentence:

3. a) Wait here. _____

   b) Have you seen an elk? _____

## SUBJECT/VERB AGREEMENT:

**Use do (don't) with I, you, or a plural subject** (more than one).
   Examples: You do*n't* have to leave.
            Raccoons do*n't* have pouches.
**Use does (doesn't) with a singular subject** (one).
   Examples: My sister does*n't* walk to school.
            He does*n't* wear glasses.
   Circle the correct word:

4. That dog ( do*n't*, does*n't* ) bite.

## SENTENCE COMBINING:

5. Jacob lost his ring.
   His ring is gold.
   It has a small red stone.

_____

_____

## CAPITALIZATION:

1. does dr. martin work at dallas children's hospital?

## PUNCTUATION:

2. Dannys dad made salad pasta and garlic bread

_____

## PREPOSITIONS AND SUBJECTS:

**Common prepositions are <u>in</u>, <u>to</u>, <u>of</u>, <u>at</u>, <u>for</u>, <u>from</u>, and <u>with</u>.**

**A prepositional phrase begins with a preposition and ends with a noun or pronoun.**

| Examples: | in the car | of sugar | at home | for us |
|---|---|---|---|---|
| | to a race | with me | on a bicycle | from dad |

**When you see a prepositional phrase in a sentence, you can cross it out. This makes finding the subject and verb easy because a word in a prepositional phrase will not be the subject or the verb.**

Example:  A cowboy went to the barn for his horse.
A cowboy went ~~to the barn for his horse~~.

Finish the prepositional phrase.

3. I met my friend **at** _____.

## SYNONYMS/ANTONYMS/HOMONYMS:

4. A homonym for <u>write</u> is _____.

## SENTENCE COMBINING:

5. Joe cut himself.
Joe needs a bandage.

_____

_____

**DAY 118**

## CAPITALIZATION:

1.  they will go to vera beach in august.

## PUNCTUATION:

2.  Tuesday May 15 2007 _____

## PREPOSITIONS AND SUBJECTS:

**Common prepositions are <u>in</u>, <u>to</u>, <u>of</u>, <u>at</u>, <u>for</u>, <u>from</u>, and <u>with</u>. A prepositional phrase begins with a preposition and ends with a noun or pronoun.**

Examples:  on a hill     of cereal     at the beach     for Kim

**When you see a prepositional phrase in a sentence, you can cross it out.  This makes finding the subject and verb easy because a word in a prepositional phrase will not be the subject or the verb.**

Example:   The card from Grandma is on the table.

**Ask yourself <u>who</u> or <u>what</u> the sentence is about.  This is the *subject*. Next, ask yourself what <u>is</u> (was) or what <u>happens</u> (happened). This is the *verb*.**

Example:   The <u>card</u> ~~from Grandma~~ <u>is</u> ~~on the table~~.

Cross out any prepositional phrases. Underline the subject once and the verb twice.

3.  Ann goes to the zoo with her class.

## SYNONYMS/ANTONYMS/HOMONYMS:

4.  A homonym for <u>meet</u> is _____.

## SENTENCE COMBINING:

5.  Her bike is a red.
    Her bike is a racer.

_____

_____

## CAPITALIZATION:

1.  have you ever fished at bulls bay in south carolina*?

    *name of a state

## PUNCTUATION:

2.  Yuck  This tastes awful _____

## PREPOSITIONS AND SUBJECTS:

> **A prepositional phrase begins with a preposition and ends with a noun or pronoun.**

>> Examples:   with my friend        on Monday        from this line

> **Cross out prepositional phrases in a sentence; this makes finding the subject and verb easy.**

>> Example:   The boy with brown hair plays in a band.

> Ask yourself who or what the sentence is about.  This is the **subject**. Next, ask yourself what is (was) or what happens (happened).  This is the **verb**.
>> Example:   The <u>boy</u> ~~with brown hair~~ <u>plays</u> ~~in a band~~.

> Cross out any prepositional phrases. Underline the subject once and the verb twice.

3.    A rabbit with brown fur hopped to our patio.

## DICTIONARY USAGE:   SYLLABLES

4.  Write a one-syllable word. _____

## SENTENCE COMBINING:

5.  Sally is on the swimming team.
    Sally is also on the diving team.


    _____


    _____

**DAY 120**

## CAPITALIZATION:

**Capitalize the name of a specific event.**

Examples:  Carnation Farmers' Market

1.  the walnut valley festival is held in winfield, kansas*.

*name of a state

## PUNCTUATION:

2.  Jacys brother hasnt moved to Reno Nevada

_____

## DIFFICULT WORDS:

**Two is the number 2.**     Example:    We have <u>two</u> pets.
**Too means *also*.**          Example:    I'm going, <u>too</u>.
**To is a preposition.**       Example:    Stay close <u>to</u> me.

Circle the correct word.

3.    Kissa wants to go, ( to, two, too ).

## PARTS OF SPEECH:   NOUNS

Write the plural of each noun.

4.  a) bench - _____       c) fizz - _____

b) dollar - _____       d) tax - _____

## SENTENCE COMBINING:

5.  Loni is angry.
Her brother won't let her play.

_____

_____

**CAPITALIZATION:**

1. many jugglers went to philly fest* in philadelphia**.
       *name of an event        **name of a city

**PUNCTUATION:**
    **Underline the title of a book.**
    **Place a short story or a poem in quotation marks (" ").**

    Examples:  a poem, "Pet Shopping"
               a story, "A Little Town Called Plink"
               a book, <u>If You Give a Mouse a Cookie</u>

2. a) a book, Fancy Nancy           c) a short story,  My Dog Nicki

   b) a poem,  I Bought a Pet Tomato

**PARTS OF SPEECH:   ADJECTIVES**

    **Adjectives are describing words.**

    Circle any adjective(s) in this sentence.

3. He has blonde hair and blue eyes.

**SUBJECT/VERB AGREEMENT:**

**The subject and verb agree in number.  If the subject is singular (one), the verb adds <u>s</u> in present time.  If the subject is plural (more than one), the verb does not add <u>s</u>.**
               Examples:  The <u>pilot</u> <u>flies</u> her plane.
                          The <u>pilots</u> <u>fly</u> their planes.

    Place two lines under the verb that agrees with the subject:

4. Each student ( walk, walks ) to school.

**SENTENCE COMBINING:**

5. Paco takes drum lessons.
   Miss Snow is his teacher.

_____

_____

## CAPITALIZATION:

**Capitalize the name of a specific building or place.**

Examples:  Hoover **D**am
Windsor **C**astle

1.  grandmother mills flew into dulles airport today.

## PUNCTUATION:

2.  Yippee  Weve won the game

_____

## PARTS OF SPEECH:   VERBS

**Verbs often show action.**

Write **A** if the verb shows action.  Do not write in the blank if the verb does not show action.

3.  a) _____ runs      (The horse runs fast.)
    b) _____ are       (You are happy.)
    c) _____ smiles    (She always smiles at me.)

## COMPOUND WORDS:
**A compound word is made up of two words.**

Example:  base  +  ball  =  baseball

4.  An example of a compound word is _____.

## SENTENCE COMBINING:

5.  Nan dropped a dime.
    Parker picked it up.

_____

_____

**CAPITALIZATION:**

1.  we saw rainbow natural bridge in arizona*.
            *name of a state

**PUNCTUATION:**

Punctuate this address.

2.  Mrs Sandy Barn

    98 Cotton Ln

    Newton NC*   28658

*When using the postal abbreviation for a state, do not use a period.

**SUBJECT/VERB:**

**The subject is *who* or *what* the sentence is about.**
    Example:   The girls swim every day.

**The verb tells what *is (was)* or what *happens (happened)*.**
    Example:   The girls swim every day.

Underline the subject once and the verb twice.

3.  Her sister always flosses.

**SYNONYMS/ANTONYMS/HOMONYMS:**

**Synonyms are words with similar meanings:  torn – ripped.**

4.  Write a synonym for skinny. _____

**SENTENCE COMBINING:**

5.  Jina is a pitcher.
    Peter is a pitcher.

**DAY 124**

## CAPITALIZATION:

**Capitalize the first word of the closing of any letter.**

1.  dear linda,
    my dad and i like the beach.
    love always,
    sarah

## PUNCTUATION:

2.  I like juice cereal and toast for breakfast

_____

## PARTS OF SPEECH:   ADJECTIVES

**<u>A</u>, <u>an</u>, and <u>the</u> are a special kind of adjective called *articles*.**

Circle these special adjectives.

3.  A moth flew through an open door.

## PARTS OF SPEECH:   NOUNS

**Most words form the plural by adding <u>s</u>.  Words ending in <u>sh</u>, <u>ch</u>, <u>s</u>, <u>x</u>, and <u>z</u> add <u>es</u> to form the plural.  <u>Some words totally change form</u>.**

Example:  one tooth  -  two teeth

Write the plural of each noun.

4. a) friend - _____      b) wish - _____      c) foot - _____

## SENTENCE COMBINING:

5.  Her skirt is blue
    Her blouse is blue, also.

_____

_____

## CAPITALIZATION:

1. has ron seen mt. everest?

## PUNCTUATION:

**Remember: An apostrophe ( ' ) is used after a noun to show possession.
If only one person or thing owns something, add 's to the noun.**

Example:   a purse that my mom owns  =  my mom's purse

2.   The dogs tail is black and white

_____

## SENTENCE TYPES:

**A statement tells something.
A question asks something.
A command tells someone to do something.**

Name the type of sentence.

3.  Did Ben buy a parrot?        _____

## PARTS OF SPEECH:   PRONOUNS

Write the correct answer on the line.

4.  (Me and Jenny, Jenny and I) _____ are going.

## SENTENCE COMBINING:

5.  Tim is holding a tennis racket.
    His uncle and aunt gave it to him.

_____

_____

**DAY 126**

## CAPITALIZATION:

1. our friend works at coach car service* in the state of ohio.

   *name of a business

## PUNCTUATION:

2. His pen pencil and pad are on the couch

_____

## PARTS OF SPEECH:   NOUNS

**A common noun names a person, place, or thing.**
**A proper noun names a specific person, place, or thing.**
**Capitalize proper nouns.**

|            | common noun |   | proper noun |
|------------|-------------|---|-------------|
| Examples:  | park        | - | **Green Park** |
|            | friend      | - | **Kala**    |

3. A beach is a common noun.  Write the name of a specific beach

   (proper noun). _____

## RHYMING WORDS:
**Rhyming words sound alike:  <u>sun</u>  -  <u>fun</u>**

4. A rhyming word for <u>time</u> is _____.

## SENTENCE COMBINING:

5. Joy ran after a ball.
   Joy fell over a chunk of wood.

_____

_____

**CAPITALIZATION:**

1.  do you take south coast highway to newport beach?

**PUNCTUATION:**

2.  His baptism was Sunday Aug 6 2006

_____

**SUBJECT/VERB AGREEMENT:**

**Present tense means now.  Form a verb in the present tense like this:**

**If the subject is singular (one), add <u>s</u> to a verb.**

**If the subject is plural (more than one), do not add s to a verb.**

Examples:   That cow **eats** slowly.
Those cows **eat** fast.

Choose the verb that agrees with the subject.

3.  His three sisters ( sing, sings ) well.

**PARTS OF SPEECH:   PRONOUNS**
**Pronouns take the place of nouns.  Some pronouns show ownership:  <u>my</u>, <u>his</u>, <u>her</u>, <u>our</u>, <u>their</u>, <u>your</u>, <u>whose</u>, and <u>its</u>.**

Write a possessive pronoun to replace the underlined words:

4.  <u>Jacob</u> and <u>Chan</u> like _____ teacher.

**SENTENCE COMBINING:**

5.  Jacy lives near an old mine.
Jenny lives near an old mine.

_____

_____

**DAY 128**

**CAPITALIZATION:**

1.  did mrs. gregg go to cape cod* in the state of massachusetts?
        *name of a cape

**PUNCTUATION:**

2.  Theyll visit on Wednesday January 17

_____


**DIFFICULT WORDS:**

3.    The bellman carried ( to, two, too ) suitcases.

**SUBJECT/VERB AGREEMENT:**

**Present tense means now.  Form a verb in the present tense like this:**

   **If the subject is singular (one), add <u>s</u> to a verb.**

   **If the subject is plural (more than one), do not add <u>s</u> to a verb.**

   **If the subject is <u>you</u> or <u>I</u>, do not add <u>s</u> to a verb.**

         Examples:    A toddler <u>plays</u> nicely.          You <u>play</u> alone.
                      Toddlers <u>play</u> together.          I <u>play</u> alone.

      Choose the verb that agrees with the subject.

4.  a)  Bo ( like, likes) corn.          b)  I ( like, likes ) corn.

**SENTENCE COMBINING:**

5.  Bart has a very sore throat.
    Bart's parents will take him to their doctor.

_____

_____

**CAPITALIZATION:**

1. last summer i went to england*.
   *name of a country

**PUNCTUATION:**

   Write the abbreviation.

2. a) street - _____     c) inch - _____

   b) September - _____   d) Saturday - _____

**PARTS OF SPEECH:   ADVERBS**
   **Do not use <u>not</u> (<u>n't</u>) and <u>nothing</u> in the same sentence.**

   Write the correct word.

3. We couldn't see _____ ( nothing, anything ).

**PARTS OF SPEECH:   NOUNS**

   **A common noun names a person, place, or thing.**
   **A proper noun names a specific person, place, or thing.**
   **Capitalize proper nouns.**

   |  | <u>common noun</u> |  | <u>proper noun</u> |
   |---|---|---|---|
   | Examples: | river | - | **S**alt **R**iver |

4. A dog is a common noun.  Write the name of a dog you know.

   The name is a proper noun. _____

**SENTENCE COMBINING:**

5. Her bracelet is made of pebbles.
   Each pebble is light green.

   _____

   _____

## CAPITALIZATION:

**Remember: Capitalize the first word when someone speaks or has spoken. This is called a direct quotation.**

Example: Kimo asked, "**W**ho are you?"

1. robby asked, "how are you?"

## PUNCTUATION:

2. No his fathers name isnt Harry

---

## PARTS OF SPEECH: PRONOUNS
**Pronouns take the place of nouns.**

Example: Pam gave **Sam** a gift.
Pam gave **him** a gift.

**Pronouns often used are <u>I</u>, <u>he</u>, <u>she</u>, <u>they</u>, <u>we</u>, <u>who</u>, <u>you</u>, <u>it</u>, and <u>me</u>, <u>him</u>, <u>her</u>, <u>them</u>, <u>us</u>, <u>whom</u>.**

3. _____ is nice.
(friend's name)

_____ is nice.
(pronoun)

## PREPOSITIONS AND SUBJECTS:
**Common prepositions are <u>after</u>, <u>at</u>, <u>by</u>, <u>in</u>, <u>for</u>, <u>from</u>, <u>to</u>, <u>on</u>, and <u>with</u>.**

**prepositional phrase =**     to     **+**     the food store
                 **preposition**          **noun** (or a pronoun)

Cross out any prepositional phrases. Then, find the subject and the verb.

4. She waits for her bus by a mailbox.

## SENTENCE COMBINING:

5. Miss Jackson smiled.
She handed me a ribbon.

---

---

**CAPITALIZATION:**

1. the man speaking french moved to lewes beach on the atlantic ocean.

**PUNCTUATION:**

   **Place an apostrophe between the o and c in o'clock.**

2. Dave Sue and Don arrived at 8 oclock

_____

**PARTS OF SPEECH:   ADVERBS**

   **Adverbs can tell when, where, and how.  They explain the verb.**

   Circle two adverbs in this sentence.

3. Come here quietly.

**SUBJECT/VERB:**

   **The subject is who or what the sentence is about.**

   **The verb is what is (was) or what happens (happened).**

   Underline the subject once and the verb twice.

4. The model smiled brightly.

**SENTENCE COMBINING:**

5. A komodo dragon is a lizard.
   It can grow to three meters long.

_____

_____

**DAY 132**

**CAPITALIZATION:**

1.  our friends went to the payson country music festival last year.

**PUNCTUATION:**

2.  Theyre meeting the salons owner at 12 30

_____

**PREPOSITIONS AND SUBJECTS:**
    **Common prepositions are <u>after</u>, <u>at</u>, <u>by</u>, <u>in</u>, <u>for</u>, <u>from</u>, <u>of</u>, <u>on</u>, <u>up</u>, and <u>with</u>. A prepositional phrase begins with a preposition and ends with a noun or pronoun.**

               Examples:   after the game      for me

    **Cross out prepositional phrases in a sentence to make finding the subject and verb easy.**
        <u>Who</u> or <u>what</u> is the sentence about?  This is the **subject**.
        What <u>is</u> <u>(was)</u> or what <u>happens</u> <u>(happened)</u>?  This is the **verb**.

        Example:   <u>Shoppers</u> <u>looked</u> ~~at clothes~~ ~~in the baby store~~.

    Cross out any prepositional phrases. Underline the subject once and the verb twice.

3.  After the game, people talked to both coaches.

**DICTIONARY USAGE:**

4.  Circle any two-syllable words:   shout    deeper    tonight    candle

**SENTENCE COMBINING:**

5.  This bat is metal.
    This bat has a baseball player's name on it.

_____

_____

## CAPITALIZATION:

1.  we have visited the glendale public library.

## PUNCTUATION:

**Place a hyphen ( - ) between two-word numbers between 21 and 99.**

Examples:  forty-one       seventy-five

2.  Peter will be twenty seven on Thursday  Feb 28

---

## PARTS OF SPEECH:   VERBS

**Use do (don't) with I, you, or a plural subject (more than one).**
Examples:   I do like iced tea.         I don't like iced tea.
They do like iced tea.      They don't live here.
**Use does (doesn't) with a singular subject (one).**
Examples:   That gardener does all the planting.
She doesn't want juice.
Circle the correct word.

3.  He ( don't, doesn't ) want to fish.

## SUBJECT/VERB:

Underline the subject once and the verb twice.

4.  He types well.

## SENTENCE COMBINING:

5.  Hannah was born in France.
Hannah's family has moved to Utah.

---

**DAY 134**

## CAPITALIZATION:

1.  ella said,  "my sister works at mama bear preschool."

## PUNCTUATION:

2.  Have you read Castle* _____
    *name of a book

## PREFIXES/ROOTS/SUFFIXES:

**A root is the main part of a word.**

**Sometimes, it is a word by itself.**
    Example:  turning  =  turn  +  ing
                           (root)      (suffix)

**Sometimes, a root is not a word by itself.**
    Example:  vision  =  **vis**  +  ion
                           (root)        (suffix)

3.  Write the root of <u>chewed</u>.  _____

## ALPHABETIZING:

4.  Write these words in alphabetical order:  limb    lace    rabbit    loan

    a) _____    b) _____    c) _____    d) _____

## SENTENCE COMBINING:

5.  Nicky has dirty hands.
    Terry has dirty hands.
    Nicky and Terry have been pulling weeds.

    _____

    _____

**CAPITALIZATION:**

1.  my dear friend,

    when will i see you again?

    always,

    ray

**PUNCTUATION:**
**Place a hyphen ( - ) between two-word numbers between 21 and 99.**
Examples:   forty-three          sixty-seven

2.  There are twenty one forks and thirty nine knives in this drawer

_____

**PARTS OF SPEECH:   NOUNS**

**Possessives:   If something that is singular (only one) shows ownership, add 's.**   Example:   one beaver's fur

Write the possessive forms.

3.  a) one boy _____ house    c)  the girl _____book

    b) a doll _____ arm

**PARTS OF SPEECH:   ADVERBS**
**Adverbs often tell where.**

Circle the adverb that tells where.

4.  Come here.

**SENTENCE COMBINING:**

5.  The chair is purple.
    It has pink stripes.

_____

_____

**DAY 136**

## CAPITALIZATION:

1. our uncle fred goes to mexico often.

## PUNCTUATION:

2. Salem  Oregon  _____
    (city)    (state)

## PREPOSITIONS AND SUBJECTS:

**A prepositional phrase begins with a preposition and ends with a noun or pronoun. <u>At</u>, <u>after</u>, <u>down</u>, <u>for</u>, <u>from</u>, <u>in</u>, <u>of</u>, <u>on</u>, <u>to</u>, <u>up</u>, and <u>with</u> are common prepositions.**

Examples:   after the movie      with us      up the stairs

**Cross out prepositional phrases.  Then, ask yourself <u>who</u> or <u>what</u> the sentence is about.  This is the subject. Next, ask yourself what <u>is</u> (was) or what <u>happens</u> (happened).  This is the verb.**

Example:   ~~After practice,~~ a few <u>players</u> <u>went</u> ~~to a diner~~.

Cross out any prepositional phrases. Underline the subject once and the verb twice.

3.   A herd of cattle roamed in the meadow.

## PARTS OF SPEECH:   INTERJECTIONS

**An interjection is a word or phrase (group of words) that shows excitement.**      Example:   Neat!

4.  Write an interjection. _____

## SENTENCE COMBINING:

5.  Her hair is wet.
    Her eyes are red.
    Her lips are turning blue.

    _____

    _____

## CAPITALIZATION:

1. yesterday, fairview bowling alley* opened.

   *name of a business

## PUNCTUATION:

2. Yes its now 2 00 _____

## PARTS OF SPEECH:   PRONOUNS

   **Pronouns take the place of nouns.**

   Place your name in the first blank.  Replace your name with a pronoun in the second blank.

3. Jim and _____ walked.

   Jim and _____ walked.

## PREFIXES/ROOTS/SUFFIXES:

   **A prefix is placed in front of a root word.  A prefix has a meaning.**

   Examples:     **un** means <u>not</u>

   **re** means <u>again</u>

4. a)   re  +  heat  =  _____

   (prefix)    (root)

   b)  What does the word mean? _____

## SENTENCE COMBINING:

5. The birthday cake has orange icing.
   The birthday cake is chocolate.

   _____

   _____

   _____

**CAPITALIZATION:**

1.  did miss borg read <u>charlotte's web</u> to you?

**PUNCTUATION:**
     Punctuate this address.

2.  Michael A Hall               _____

     57 Linx Ave                    _____

     Tulsa OK   74133          _____

**PARTS OF SPEECH:   NOUNS**

**A common noun names a person, place, or thing.**
**A proper noun names a specific person, place, or thing.**
**Capitalize proper nouns.**

|  | <u>common noun</u> |  | <u>proper noun</u> |
|---|---|---|---|
| Example: | highway | - | **B**lue **S**tar **H**ighway |
|  | child | - | **A**ndy |

3.  A sea is a common noun.  Write the name of a specific sea (proper

     noun).  _____

**DIFFICULT WORDS:**

     **You're is a contraction for *you are*.**    Example:  <u>You're</u> correct!

     **Your is a pronoun.**    Example:  We like <u>your</u> family.

     Circle the correct word.

4.  ( Your, You're ) the winner!

**SENTENCE COMBINING:**

5.  The taxi driver slowed.
     A lady crossed the street.


     _____

     _____

**CAPITALIZATION:**

**In a title, capitalize the first word, the last word, and all important words. Do not capitalize <u>a</u>, <u>an</u>, <u>the</u>, <u>and</u>, <u>but</u>, <u>or</u>, or <u>nor</u> *unless* they are the first or last word.**

1. her story was called "the cat and the joey."

**PUNCTUATION:**

**Remember: Place a comma after the person to whom you are speaking.**

2. Ben may I go with you _____

**PREFIXES/ROOTS/SUFFIXES:**

**A root is the main part of a word.**
**Sometimes, it is a word by itself.**
    Example: return = re + **turn**
                   (prefix)    (root)

**Sometimes, a root is not a word by itself.**
    Example: scribble = **scrib** + ble
                   (root)    (suffix)

3. What is the root of <u>sickness</u>? _____

**SUBJECT/VERB:**

**The subject tells <u>who</u> or <u>what</u> the sentence is about.**
**The verb often shows action.**

Underline the subject once and the verb twice.

4. Her cat purred softly.

**SENTENCE COMBINING:**

5. This bag is large.
   We will put food into it.

_____

_____

**DAY 140**

## CAPITALIZATION:

1. tomorrow, i will read "herbie rides again."

## PUNCTUATION:

2. We arrived at 10 30 on Friday Oct 23

_____

## PARTS OF A BOOK:   TABLE OF CONTENTS

**A table of contents is at the beginning of a book.
It tells chapters (and/or units) in the book.**

|  | *Chapter Number* | *Title of Chapter* | *Page Number* |
|---|---|---|---|
| Example: | Chapter 1 | Worms.................................5 |  |
|  | Chapter 2 | Frogs..............................16 |  |
|  | Chapter 3 | Toads...............................25 |  |

3. On what page will you turn to find a chapter about toads? _____

## PARTS OF SPEECH:   ADJECTIVES

**Some adjectives describe.**

Find two adjectives that describe.

4. Pretty flowers are planted under a maple tree.

## SENTENCE COMBINING:

5. Lightning flashed.
Thunder boomed.
There was a storm.

_____

_____

_____

**CAPITALIZATION:**

1.  janet gobb travels to lake erie every summer.

**PUNCTUATION:**

> **Underline the title of a book.  Place the title of a story, poem, song, or chapter in quotation marks (" ").**
> > Example:   the book, <u>Flutterby</u>
> > the song, "If You're Happy and You Know It"

2.  Sandy have you read the book, Half of an Elephant

---

**PARTS OF SPEECH:   NOUNS**
> **A noun names a person, place, or thing.**

> Find two nouns that name <u>things</u>.

3.  His ball rolled under the sofa.

**DICTIONARY:   GUIDE WORDS**
> **Two guide words are written at the top of each dictionary page.**
> **The first word tells you the first word listed on the page.**
> **The other word across from it tells you the last word on that page.**
> > Example:   **icy**                              **inner**

4.  Will the word <u>ill</u> be on the page with the guide words <u>icy</u> and <u>inner</u>?_____

**SENTENCE COMBINING:**

5.  Jack wants pizza for lunch.
    Jana wants a tuna salad for lunch.

_____

_____

**DAY 142**

## CAPITALIZATION:
Capitalize this friendly letter.

1. dear anna,

    come to see me soon.

        love,

        betsy

## PUNCTUATION:

2. Orlando Florida _____
   (city)     (state)

## PARTS OF SPEECH:   NOUNS
**Plural means more than one.  Most words add s to make the plural.**

**If a word ends in a vowel + y (ay, ey, oy, or uy), adds s.**  Example:   days

**If a word ends with a consonant + y, the plural is made by changing y**

**to i and adding es.**        Example:   sky - skies

Write the plural of each noun.

3.   a) baby - _____        b) boy - _____

## PARTS OF SPEECH:   PRONOUNS
**Pronouns take the place of nouns.  Some pronouns show ownership:  my, his, her, our, their, your, whose, and its.**

Write a possessive pronoun to replace the underlined words.

4. My mom and I like nuts on _____ banana splits.

## SENTENCE COMBINING:

5. Their sister is thirteen.
   Their sister likes to skate.

   _____

   _____

**CAPITALIZATION:**

1. did you see niagara falls* in the state of new york?

    *name of a place

**PUNCTUATION:**

2. The play will be Tuesday Feb 4

_____

**PARTS OF SPEECH:   PREPOSITIONS**

**Common prepositions are <u>to</u>, <u>for</u>, <u>at</u>, <u>from</u>, <u>in</u>, <u>on</u>, <u>up</u>, and <u>down</u>.**

**A prepositional phrase begins with a preposition and stops with**

**a noun (or pronoun like *me*).**   Example:  **from** my friend

Cross out the prepositional phrase that begins with <u>from</u>.

3. The package from Grandma arrived.

**RHYMING WORDS:**

4. A word that rhymes with <u>book</u> is _____.

**SENTENCE COMBINING:**

5. Their grammy has blue eyes.
   She has blonde hair.
   She lives in Delaware.

_____

_____

_____

**DAY 144**

## CAPITALIZATION:

Remember: **Capitalize the name of specific geographic places.**
**Capitalize street and highway names. Capitalize names of town (cities).**
**Capitalize the postal code for each state.**

Examples: **Ray Street**       **San Diego**
**Mammoth Cave**   **Minnesota = MN**

Capitalize this address:

1.   mr. john i. sarter

918 north maple street

upper saddle river, nj    07458

## PUNCTUATION:

2.   A cows tail is very long  _____

## PREFIXES/ROOTS/SUFFIXES:

**A root is the main part of a word.**       Example:   kind
**A prefix is placed in front of a root.**   Example:   **un**kind
**A suffix is placed at the end of a word.** Example:   kind**ness**
Fill in the blanks.

3.   repainting  = _____ (prefix) + _____ (root) + _____ (suffix)

## DICTIONARY:   GUIDE WORDS

**There are two guide words listed at the top on each dictionary page.**
**The first word tells you the first word listed on the page.**
**The word across from it tells you the last word on the page.**
Example:   **garbage**                      **great**

4.   Will <u>gate</u> be on the page with the guide words, <u>garbage</u> and <u>great</u>?  _____

## SENTENCE COMBINING:

5.   Snow has fallen.
Everyone is sledding.


_____

_____

## CAPITALIZATION:

**Remember:  Capitalize the first word, the last word, and all important words in a title.**

1.  the book named <u>jillian jigs</u> was written by phoebe gilman.


## PUNCTUATION:

**Remember:   If a word that is singular (one) shows ownership, add <u>'s</u>.**
         Example:   food for one rabbit  =  one rabbit**'s** food

**If a word that is plural (more than one) shows ownership, add <u>s'</u>.**
         Example:   food for two rabbits  =  rabbits' food

2.  Ann have you seen these girls mother

_____


## ALPHABETIZING:

3.  Write these words in alphabetical order:   up     lift     pony     ladder

   a) _____     b) _____     c) _____     d) _____


## PARTS OF SPEECH:   NOUNS

**Plural means more than one.  Most words add <u>s</u> to form the plural.
If a word ends in a vowel + <u>y</u>, adds <u>s</u>.** Example:  pl<u>ay</u> - pl<u>ay</u>**s**

**If a word ends with a consonant + <u>y</u>, the plural is formed by changing
<u>y</u> to <u>i</u> and adding <u>es</u>.**         Example:   past<u>ry</u> - past<u>ri</u>**es**

Write the plural of each noun.

4.   a) key - _____          b) bunny - _____


## SENTENCE COMBINING:

5.  The chest is made of oak.
    The chest belongs to Mrs. Karn.

_____

_____

## CAPITALIZATION:

**Capitalize our country or a describing word that comes from our country.**
Example:   America   -   American

1.   an american flag is flying at mayfair school.

## PUNCTUATION:

Punctuate these abbreviations.

2.   a)   foot = ft          b)   yard = yd          c)   Doctor = Dr

## SUBJECT/VERB AGREEMENT:

**The subject and verb agree in number.  If the subject is singular, the verb will add <u>s</u> in present time.  If the subject is plural (more than one), the verb will not add <u>s</u>.**
Examples:   The <u>boy</u> <u>likes</u> to climb.
The <u>boys</u> <u>like</u> to climb.

Place two lines under the verb that agrees with the subject.

3.   Janice ( chews, chew ) her food slowly.

## PARTS OF SPEECH:   ADJECTIVES
<u>A</u>, <u>an</u>, and <u>the</u> are special kinds of adjectives called *articles*.

Circe the special adjectives called articles.

4.   The group went to an old inn in a little village.

## SENTENCE COMBINING:

5.   Larry's favorite dessert is berry pie.
My favorite dessert is fruit salad.

_____

_____

## CAPITALIZATION:
**Capitalize the first word in an outline.**

Example:  I.  **F**rogs and toads
II.  **L**izards

1.  I.  flowers
II.  trees and bushes

## PUNCTUATION:
**Place someone's exact words in quotation marks.**
**Place a comma after the name of the person speaking +** *said* **(or** *asked***).**
**Place the end punctuation mark inside the quotation marks.**

Example:  **Betty said,** "I can't find my keys."

2.  Joe said  Look here  _____

## PARTS OF SPEECH:  NOUNS
**A common noun names a person, place, or thing.**
Examples:  park        school
**A proper noun names a particular person, place, or thing.**
**Capitalize a proper noun.**

Examples:  park (common)  -  **P**enn **P**ark  (proper)
school (common)  -  **S**unrise **E**lementary **S**chool  (proper)

Write **C** if the noun is common and **P** is the noun is proper.

3.  a)  _____ lake                c)  _____ town
b)  _____ Lake Todd           d)  _____ Brownville

## RHYMING WORDS:

4.  A rhyming word for <u>back</u> is  _____.

## SENTENCE COMBINING:

5.  Jana's knee is sore.
Her ankle and foot are sore.

_____

_____

**DAY 148**

**CAPITALIZATION:**

1.   we celebrate independence day* on july 4.
*name of a special day

**PUNCTUATION:**

2.   Sarah asked  Are you sure

_____

**PARTS OF SPEECH:   ADJECTIVES**

**When you are comparing two items using a one-syllable adjective (describing word), add er.**
Example:   (small)  Your ball is small, but this ball is small**er**.

**When you are comparing three or more items using a one-syllable adjective (describing word), add est.**
Example:   (small)  Of the three balls, this one is small**est**.

Write the correct adjective.

3.   This book is short, but that one is _____.

**PARTS OF SPEECH:   ADVERBS**

**Adverbs tell how, when, and where.**

Circle any adverbs.

4.   We will sleep late tomorrow.

**SENTENCE COMBINING:**

5.   The leaves have changed color.
It is autumn.

_____

_____

## CAPITALIZATION:
Capitalize this friendly letter.

1.  dear mrs. winston,

    we will see you on sunday, november 4

    your friend,

    lucy

## PUNCTUATION:

2.  Davids dad was born on Oct 12  1965

_____

## PARTS OF A BOOK:   INDEX
**An index is located at the end of a book.**
**The index tells where (which page) to turn for information about a topic.**
**The number after the topic is the page.**
Example:   Bats, 27
Birds, 12
Bugs, 126
You can find information about bats on page 27 (Bats, 27).

3.  On what page can you find information about bugs? _____

## SUBJECT/VERB:

**A subject tells who or what a sentence is about.**
**A verb often shows action.**

Place one line under the subject and two lines under the verb.

4.  Her aunt drives a tractor.

## SENTENCE COMBINING:

5.  A squirrel gathers nuts for the winter.
    A squirrel stores nuts for the winter.

_____

_____

## CAPITALIZATION:

**Capitalize the first word, the last word, and all important words in a title. Do not capitalize <u>a</u>, <u>an</u>, <u>the</u>, <u>and</u>, <u>but</u>, <u>or</u>, <u>nor</u>, or prepositions of four or less letters (<u>to</u>, <u>for</u>, <u>from</u>, <u>in</u>, <u>at</u>, <u>down</u>) *unless* they are the first or last word.**     Example:   "The **B**oy in the **B**oat"

Capitalize these titles.

1.  a)  <u>bunnicula</u>          b)  <u>jack in the beanstalk</u>

## PUNCTUATION:

2.  They havent been to Dade City Florida

_____

## PARTS OF A BOOK:   TABLE OF CONTENTS

**A table of contents is located at the beginning of a book.  It gives titles and page numbers telling where each chapter begins.  It also tells where maps, the index, glossary (dictionary), and other useful information begin.**

|            | Chapter Number | Title of Chapter | Page Number |
|------------|----------------|------------------|-------------|
| Example:   | Chapter 1      | Early America    | 2           |
|            | Chapter 2      | Colonists        | 16          |
|            |                | Maps             | 25          |
|            |                | Glossary         | 46          |

3.   To which page will you turn to look for a word in the glossary? _____

## DIFFICULT WORDS:

Circle the correct word.

4.   Where is ( their, there, they're ) dad?

## SENTENCE COMBINING:

5.   Jana played soccer.
     Then, she went to a music store.

_____

_____

## CAPITALIZATION:

**Remember:   Capitalize a person's title when it appears with a name.**
Examples:   **M**ayor Jones      **C**aptain Smith      **A**unt Lisa

1.   was president madison born in the united states?

## PUNCTUATION:

2.   Yeah  Lets go _____

## DIFFICULT WORDS:

**it's  =  it is**
**Its shows ownership.**    Example:   The cat licked **its** paw.
If you are not sure which to use, try reading the sentence with the <u>it's</u> form.
The cat licked <u>it is</u> paw.
Of course, this is wrong.  Also, **its** shows that the paw belongs to the cat.

**To is a preposition (to the store).**
**Two is the number 2.**
**Too means also or a very great amount.**

Write the correct word.

3.    a)   ( It's, Its ) _____ time to eat.
      b)   We want to swing, _____ ( to, two, too ).

## PARTS OF SPEECH:   NOUNS
**Nouns name persons, places, and things.**
Circe the nouns.

4.   These keys belong to a dentist from Texas.

## SENTENCE COMBINING:

5.   Mrs. Cod works in a card shop.
Her daughter works in the same shop.

_____

_____

**DAY 152**

## CAPITALIZATION:

1.  the brooks family went to flathead lake in montana*.

                              *name of a state

## PUNCTUATION:

2.  Kim youre a good football and tennis player

---

## PARTS OF SPEECH:  ADJECTIVES

A, an, and the are special adjectives called articles.
Some adjectives tell what kind.        Example:    *red* shoes
Some adjectives tell which one(s).     Example:    *this* crayon
Some adjectives tell how many.         Example:    *several* boats

Circle any adjectives.

3.  Some small red cherries are in a tin bucket.

## PARTS OF SPEECH:  VERBS

Verbs tell what is (was) or what happens (happened).
Sometimes, a sentence contains two verbs.
This is called a compound verb.
        Example:    They jumped up and ran.

Find the compound verb in the following sentence. (What did Jack do?)

4.  Jack washed and dried his hands.

## SENTENCE COMBINING:

5.  Misha paints pictures.
    Misha's pictures are of animals.
    Misha sells them, too.

---

---

## CAPITALIZATION:

1. a) <u>noah's ark</u>        b) <u>lost horizon</u>

## PUNCTUATION:

**Place a period after each number or letter in an outline.**
    Example:  I. Lakes
                    A. Large lakes
                    B. Small lakes
            II. Seas

Punctuate this outline.

2. I Trees        _____
    A Birch      _____
    B Pine       _____
II Bushes        _____

## PARTS OF SPEECH:   ADJECTIVES

**When you are comparing 2 things using a one-syllable adjective**
(describing word), **use er.**        Example:   This glass is tall**er** than that one.

**When you are comparing 3 or more things using a one-syllable adjective**
(describing word), **use est.**        Example:   This glass is tall**est** of the three.

Write the correct adjective.

3. a) Of the two poles, this one is ( taller, tallest ) _____.
    b) She is ( taller, tallest ) _____ of the four children.

## CONJUNCTIONS:

Unscramble these conjunctions.

4. a) ro - _____    b) nda - _____    c) utb - _____

## SENTENCE COMBINING:

5. A goat is standing high on a cliff.
    It is a mountain goat.

_____

_____

**CAPITALIZATION:**

1.  their address is 3 park lane.

**PUNCTUATION:**
   **Underline the titles of books, movies, and plays.**
   **Place titles of stories, poems, and songs in quotation marks.**

   Punctuate these titles.

2.  a) (poem)  The Crocodile's Toothache  _____

   b) (story)  Sleeping Beauty  _____

   c) (book)  Mrs. Pigglewiggle  _____

**PARTS OF SPEECH:   NOUNS**
   **By definition, common nouns do not name a specific person, place, or thing.  Most nouns are common nouns.**
   Examples:  man          store          ocean

   **By definition, proper nouns do name a specific person, place, or thing.  Capitalize all proper nouns.**
   Examples:  Tom          Coe Bakery     Atlantic Ocean
   Write a proper noun for each common noun.

3.  a)  store - _____          b)  woman - _____

**PARTS OF SPEECH:   NOUNS**
   **Plural means more than one.  If a word ends in a consonant + y, change the y to i and add es.**     Example:   one buddy  -  two buddies

   **Plural means more than one.  If a word ends in a vowel + y, add s.**
   Example:   one donkey  -  two donkeys
   Write the plural of each noun.

4.  a)  stray - _____          b)  berry - _____

**SENTENCE COMBINING:**

5.  Zoey sanded the floor in her living room.
   Zoey stained the floor in her living room.

   _____

   _____

## CAPITALIZATION:

1. during the winter, senator owens flew to dallas, texas.
   <sub>(city)</sub>     <sub>(state)</sub>

## PUNCTUATION:

2. Well live at 12 Main Street Atlanta Georgia
   <sub>(city)</sub>     <sub>(state)</sub>

_____

## SENTENCE TYPES:

**A statement tells something and ends in a period ( . ). This is also called a *declarative* sentence.**    Example: They eat lunch early.
**A question asks something and ends with a question mark ( ? ). This is also called an *interrogative* sentence.**    Example: Do you eat ice?
**A command tells someone to do something and ends in a period ( . ). This is also called an *imperative* sentence.**   Example: Please stop.
**An exclamatory sentence tells something with excitement. It ends in an exclamation point ( ! ).**    Example: I love it!

Name these sentence types.

3. a) Give this to your mother. _____
   b) Will you give this to your mother? _____

## PARTS OF SPEECH:  PRONOUNS
**Pronouns take the place of nouns.**
**Pronouns:  <u>I</u>, <u>he</u>, <u>she</u>, <u>we</u>, <u>they</u>, <u>who</u>,**
          **<u>me</u>, <u>him</u>, <u>her</u>, <u>us</u>, <u>them</u>, <u>whom</u>, <u>you</u>, and <u>it</u>.**
Replace the underlined word with a pronoun.

4. Ander and <u>Ann</u> are having fun.
   Ander and _____ are having fun.

## SENTENCE COMBINING:

5. Take your papers from your backpack.
   Give them to Ms. Dell.

_____

_____

**DAY 156**

**CAPITALIZATION:**

1.  is wayne national forest in southern ohio*?
    *name of a state

**PUNCTUATION:**

Write each abbreviation.

2.  a) Saturday - _____     c) December - _____

    b) Avenue - _____     d) quart - _____

**PARTS OF SPEECH:   ADVERBS**

**Adverbs often tell <u>when</u> or <u>where</u>.**

Circle any adverbs that tell <u>when</u> or <u>where</u>.

3.  We will walk around later.

**PARTS OF SPEECH:   INTERJECTIONS**

**An interjection is a word or phrase (group of words) that shows excitement.**

Example:  Yikes!

4.  Write an interjection. _____

**SENTENCE COMBINING:**

5.  Starvine Ranch is a working ranch.
    Horses are raised there.

_____

_____

## CAPITALIZATION:
**Do not capitalize *said* or *asked* after the words spoken by someone.**
Example: "Don't move," **s**aid Paco.

1. "has uncle mack come to the carnival?" asked anna.

## PUNCTUATION:

2. Her new address is 203 Frog Avenue Highland Park Illinois

_____

## PARTS OF SPEECH:    CONJUNCTIONS

**Conjunctions are connecting words.**

Write the conjunctions.

3. a)  a _ _          b) b _ _          c) o _

Use a conjunction in this sentence.

d)  Wendy is eating an apple _____ a banana.

## SUBJECT:
**The subject of a sentence tells <u>who</u> or <u>what</u> the sentence is about. Sometimes, there is more than one subject. This is called a compound subject.**

Underline the compound subject.

4. A baker and her helper made cookies.

## SENTENCE COMBINING:

5. The movie began.
Everyone took a seat.

_____

_____

## CAPITALIZATION:

**Capitalize the first word, the last word, and all important words in a title. Do not capitalize <u>a</u>, <u>an</u>, <u>the</u>, <u>and</u>, <u>but</u>, <u>or</u>, <u>nor</u>, or prepositions of four or less letters (<u>to</u>, <u>for</u>, <u>from</u>, <u>in</u>, <u>at</u>, <u>down</u>) *unless* they are the first or last word.**

Capitalize these book titles.

1.  a)  <u>good boy, fergus</u>

    b)  <u>ella sarah gets dressed</u>

    c)  <u>a chair for my mother</u>

## PUNCTUATION:

2.  Yes were giving Trenas friend a balloon

_____

## PARTS OF SPEECH:   ADVERBS

**Do not use <u>not</u> and <u>nothing</u> in the same sentence.**

Write the correct word.

3.   I do not know _____ ( nothing, anything ).

## PARTS OF SPEECH:   VERBS

**Past tense means something has already happened.  Most verbs add <u>ed</u> to form the past tense.  These are called *regular verbs*.  Example:  Bo <u>meowed</u>. Some verbs called *irregular verbs* do not add <u>ed</u>; they change form to tell past time.     Example:  Rob <u>**wrote**</u> a letter.**

Write the past tense.

4.  a) (to wave)  She _____.    b) (to sing)  She _____

## SENTENCE COMBINING:

5.  The basketball team ran onto the court.
    The fans cheered.

_____

_____

**CAPITALIZATION:**

1.   dr. a. j. smith said, "a meeting will be held in the summer."

**PUNCTUATION:**

2.   That pens stripes are red blue and green

_____

**PARTS OF SPEECH:   VERBS**
  **Past tense means something has already happened.**
  **Most verbs are *regular* and add <u>ed</u>.**    Example:  Rena <u>smil**ed**</u>.
  **Some verbs called *irregular verbs* change form to tell past time.**
     Example:  <u>Jacob **swam**</u> in a lake.

  Write the past tense.

3.  a) to chew  -  A goat _____.    b) to sit  -  We _____.

**PARTS OF SPEECH:   NOUNS**
  Write the plural of each noun:

4.   a)  bus - _____     c)  puppy - _____

     b)  paper - _____     d)  mouse - _____

**SENTENCE COMBINING:**

5.   Troy sent a card.
     The card was a Valentine's card.
     He sent it to his wife.

_____

_____

## CAPITALIZATION:

**Do not capitalize the name of a subject in school unless it is a language or has a number with it.**

Example:    He likes reading and **E**nglish.

1.  does lee like spanish or math better at deep river school?


## PUNCTUATION:

Write the abbreviation.

2.  a) Sunday- \_\_\_\_\_     b) Road- \_\_\_\_\_     c) August- \_\_\_\_\_     d) feet- \_\_\_\_\_


## PARTS OF SPEECH:   PREPOSITIONS

**A prepositional phrase is a group of words that begin with a preposition. Usually, it ends with something you can see.  Common prepositions: <u>at</u>, <u>in</u>, <u>to</u>, <u>for</u>, <u>from</u>, <u>with</u>, <u>up</u>, and <u>down</u>.**        Examples: in the *road*   with *me*

Cross out any prepositional phrases.

3.  Jana went with her friends to the store.


## FRIENDLY LETTER:

**The parts of a friendly letter are:**

3 Colonial Avenue
York, PA  17403                                    **(heading)**
May 7, 20—

Dear Tama,                                            **(greeting)**
    We will meet you in Scranton soon.       **(message  or body)**
                Your cousin,                          **(closing)**
                Tate                                       **(signature)**

Write the part of the friendly letter.

4.    a)  Dear Tama, _____
      b)  We will meet you in Scranton soon. _____
      c)  Your cousin, _____
      d)  Tate _____


## SENTENCE COMBINING:

5.  The light is bright.
    It shines in my window.


_____


_____

## CAPITALIZATION:

1. "we have crossed the mississippi river," said fran.

## PUNCTUATION:

Punctuate this friendly letter.

2.                              111 East Brell Dr          _____

   (heading)                   Atlantic City  NJ          _____

                               March 3 20—                _____

(greeting)        Dear Miss Than _____

(body or message)      Yes I will come at 8 45 _____

        (closing)               Love                       _____

        (signature)             Mandy

## PARTS OF SPEECH:   ADVERBS

**There are 7 common adverbs that tell <u>to what extent</u>:
<u>not</u>, <u>so</u>, <u>very</u>, <u>too</u>, <u>quite</u>, <u>rather</u>, and <u>somewhat</u>.**

Circle any adverbs that tell <u>to what extent</u>.

3. Gina is quite active and so funny.

## PARTS OF SPEECH:   PRONOUNS

**Pronouns take the place of nouns.  Some pronouns show
ownership: <u>my</u>, <u>his</u>, <u>her</u>, <u>our</u>, <u>their</u>, <u>your</u>, <u>whose</u>, and <u>its</u>.**

Circle any possessive pronoun:

4. Do you like your new toy?

## SENTENCE COMBINING:

5. David is moving.
   David is moving next spring.
   David is moving to New York.

_____

_____

**DAY 162**

## CAPITALIZATION:
Capitalize these titles.

1. a) <u>the stray dog</u>

   b) "the army of two"

   c) <u>family circle</u>

   d) "make way for wanda"

## PUNCTUATION:

**Remember:  If 2 describing words come in front of something (noun or pronoun) and one describing word is a number or color, do not place a comma between the 2 describing words.**

Examples:   a large white dog
four little kittens

2. Mandys small brown dog isnt a bulldog

_____

## PARTS OF SPEECH:   CONJUNCTIONS
**Conjunctions are joining words.**
**Common conjunctions are <u>and</u>, <u>but</u>, and <u>or</u>.**

Use a conjunction that makes sense.

3. Butter is rich, _____ margarine has fewer calories.

## SUBJECT:
**The subject of a sentence tells <u>who</u> or <u>what</u> the sentence is about. Sometimes, there is more than one subject.  This is called a compound subject.**

Underline the compound subject.

4. That tall, strong man and his partner move furniture.

## SENTENCE COMBINING:

5. Dreena twirls her baton.
   Dreena marches in a band.

_____

_____

## CAPITALIZATION:

1.  in july, we went to merrimac caverns*.
    *name of a particular place

## PUNCTUATION:
**Place a period after <u>Ms.</u>, a title for a female.**
Punctuate this friendly letter.

2.                              678 Johnson St            _____

    (heading)                  Gettysburg PA  17325      _____

                               February 7 2009           _____

(greeting)        Dear Ms Little  _____

(body or message)     Our plane will arrive at 2 15  _____

        (closing)              Truly yours _____

        (signature)            Koko

## FRIENDLY LETTER:

3.  What is written on the third line of a heading? _____

## SYNONYMS/ANTONYMS/HOMONYMS:
**Antonyms are words with opposite meanings.**

4.  An antonym for <u>top</u> is _____.

## SENTENCE COMBINING:

5.  Sissy likes to swing.
    She swings at a playground in the park.

    _____

    _____

    _____

**DAY 164**

**CAPITALIZATION:**

1.   joy j. jones is a teacher at penn middle school.


**PUNCTUATION:**
 **Place a comma after the person speaking + *exclaimed* or *said* or *asked*.**

            Example:   Jana exclaimed, **"Hi! I'm here!"**

2.   Miss Clegg exclaimed   You are the winner

_____


**SUBJECT/VERB:**
     **A subject tells <u>who</u> or <u>what</u> the sentence is about.**
     **A verb often shows action.**

     Underline the subject once and the verb twice.

3.    A driver yelled to his friend.


**PARTS OF SPEECH:   NOUNS**
     **Plural means more than one.**
     **Add <u>es</u> to form the plural of words ending in <u>sh</u>, <u>ch</u>, <u>s</u>, <u>x</u>, and <u>z</u>.**
     **If a word ends in a consonant + <u>y</u>, change the <u>y</u> to <u>i</u> and add <u>es</u>.**
     **If a word ends in a vowel + <u>y</u> (<u>ay</u>, <u>ey</u>, <u>uy</u>, or <u>oy</u>), just add <u>s</u>.**

     Write the plural of each noun:

4.   a)  coach - _____      c)  baggy - _____

     b)  fence - _____      d)  bay - _____


**SENTENCE COMBINING:**

5.   Their scout troop will meet on Monday.
     Their scout troop will meet at Marco's house.

     _____

     _____

     _____

## CAPITALIZATION:

1. is this the continent of north america?


## PUNCTUATION:

**If two describing words (adjectives) come before a noun, place a comma between them. If one of the adjectives is a color or a number, do not use a comma.**

Examples:     a large, icy drink
a small red ball
five pretty flowers

2. A tall famous arch is in St Louis Missouri
                             (city)      (state)

_____


## DICTIONARY:   GUIDE WORDS

**Guide words tell you the first word and the last word on a dictionary page.**

Example:     **girl**          **gobble**

3. Will the word <u>glad</u> be found on a dictionary page with the guide words, <u>girl</u> and <u>gobble</u>? _____


## ADJECTIVE OR ADVERB?:

<u>Good</u> **is an adjective that describes:** good game. ***Good* describes *game* (noun).**
<u>Well</u> **is an adverb that tells *how* someone does something.** He swims well.

Write the correct word.

4. a)  Gail is a _____ player.     b)  Gail plays _____.


## SENTENCE COMBINING:

5. The cookies burned.
The cookies were in the oven too long.


_____

_____

**DAY 166**

## CAPITALIZATION:
Capitalize this heading and greeting of a friendly letter.

1.                                                 3627 north allen drive
                                                   lubbock, tx    79407
                                                   june 2, 20—

     dear aunt carole,

## PUNCTUATION:

**If one person or thing owns something, add 's.**
**If two or more own something and the noun ends in <u>s</u>, add '.**
    Examples:   one duck's feathers
                many ducks' pond

2.  His three cousins scooter is broken

---

## SUBJECT/VERB AGREEMENT:
**Use do (don't) with <u>I</u>, <u>you</u>, or <u>a plural subject</u>** (more than one).
    Example:   The climbers do*n't* have ropes.
**Use does (doesn't) with <u>a singular subject</u> (one).**
    Example:   She does*n't* sew.
Circle the correct word.

3.  He ( do*n't*, does*n't* ) like onions.

## PARTS OF SPEECH:   ADJECTIVES
**Adjectives are describing words.**

Circle 2 adjectives that describe kitchens.

4.   Kitchens can be neat or messy.

## SENTENCE COMBINING:

5.  Some puppies were playing together.
    The puppies were energetic.

---

---

## CAPITALIZATION:

1. the rangers' club will meet at south mountain fairgrounds today.

## PUNCTUATION:
**Underline the titles of books, magazines, movies, and plays.**
**Place titles of stories, poems, and songs in quotation marks.**

Punctuate these titles.

2. a) a book, Stone Fox      _____

   b) a story, The Lost Colony      _____

   c) a magazine, Animal Fun      _____

## SUBJECT/VERB:
**The subject of a sentence tells <u>who</u> or <u>what</u> the sentence is about.**
**Sometimes, there is more than one subject.**
**This is called a compound subject.**

Underline the compound subject.

3. A swan and a large duck swim on the pond.

## DICTIONARY: SYLLABLES
**Words have different units of sound called syllables. Some words say just one sound. These are called one-syllable words.** Example: car

**Some words are made up of more than one sound. We can divide them into units of sound.**
         Examples: ap ple     bas ket ball
Divide these words into syllables.

4. a) baby - _____     b) Saturday - _____

## SENTENCE COMBINING:

5. His first airplane flight was to Denver.
   Denver is in Colorado.

   _____

   _____

**CAPITALIZATION:**

1.  the spanish class went to mexico city last july.

**PUNCTUATION:**

2.  A small peppy puppy licked its paws

---

**PARTS OF SPEECH:   ADVERBS**

> **Some words are called negative words.**
> **Some negative words are <u>no</u>, <u>not</u>, <u>never</u>, and <u>none</u>.**
> **Do not use two negatives in the same sentence.**

3.  Ken never has _____ ( any, no ) time for cartoons.

**PARTS OF SPEECH:   PRONOUNS**
> **Pronouns take the place of nouns.**
> **Pronouns:  <u>I</u>, <u>he</u>, <u>she</u>, <u>we</u>, <u>they</u>, <u>who</u>,**
> **<u>me</u>, <u>him</u>, <u>her</u>, <u>us</u>, <u>them</u>, <u>whom</u>, <u>you</u>, and <u>it</u>.**

   Replace the underlined noun(s) with a pronoun:

4.  a)  <u>Dr. Minter</u> is here.
   _____ is here.

   b)  <u>Kim</u> and <u>Terry</u> are friends.
   _____ are friends.

**SENTENCE COMBINING:**

5.  Lacy bought a pin for her mom.
   Lacy bought a pen for her dad.
   Lacy bought a toy for her brother.

---

---

**CAPITALIZATION:**

1. is everglades national park in florida?

**PUNCTUATION:**
 **This may help you to punctuate titles:**
 **If it is a large item that can be received in the mail, you usually underline the title.**
 Examples: a book, <u>Old Yeller</u>
 a magazine, <u>Teen Talk</u>
 **If it is a small item like a chapter in a book, you usually place the title in quotation marks.** Examples: a poem, "Butterflies"
 a short story, "A Funny Day"

 Punctuate these titles.

2. a) book, Submarines _____

 b) school report, Lions and Tigers _____

 c) chapter, Our Muscles _____

**PARTS OF SPEECH: VERBS**
 **Tense means time. Past tense tells what happened.**
 **Future tense tells what will happen.**

3. a) Yesterday, Josh _____ (to go) to a water park.
 b) Next week, Josh _____ (to go) to Bull Lake.

**SENTENCE TYPES:**
 **A statement tells something.** (declarative)
 **A question asks something.** (interrogative)
 **A command says to do something.** (imperative)
 **An exclamatory sentence says something with emotion.**

 Name the type of sentence.

4. a) Take this home. _____

**SENTENCE COMBINING:**

5. Chan likes to play football.
 Chan does not like to run laps.

 _____

 _____

**DAY 170**

**CAPITALIZATION:**

1.  their sister yelled,  "we're going to the mummasburg baseball festival!"

**PUNCTUATION:**
    Punctuate these titles.

2.  a)  (book)  The Contest _____

    b)  (poem)  My Bug _____

    c)  (song)  Yankee Doodle _____

**PARTS OF SPEECH:   ADJECTIVES**
    **Adjectives are describing words.**  Example:   *little* girl
    **Some adjectives are called limiting adjectives. <u>This</u>, <u>that</u>, <u>those</u>,
    and <u>these</u> are limiting adjectives.**   Example:   *that* picture
    Fill in each blank with a limiting adjective.

3.  a) _____ shirt is dirty.    b) Kirk likes _____ shoes.

**PARTS OF SPEECH:   NOUNS**
    **Some nouns do not add <u>s</u> or <u>es</u> to form the plural.**
    **Some totally change.**   Example:   one **foot**  -  two **feet**
    **Some do not change at all.**   Example:   one **deer**  -  many **deer**
    **Use a dictionary if you are not sure of a plural.  *Pl* means plural.**
    **If no plural is given, you usually add <u>s</u>.**

4.  a) child -_____  b) tooth -_____  c) moose -_____

**SENTENCE COMBINING:**

5.  We blew up balloons for a party.
    The party is for Jimmy's birthday.
    It is for Jimmy's first birthday.

    _____

    _____

    _____

## CAPITALIZATION:

1. will mr. and mrs. cline visit morro bay?

## PUNCTUATION:

2. Chan asked  Arent Rick Frisco and Jacy coming

---

## PARTS OF A BOOK:   INDEX

**An index is located at the end of a book.**
**The index tells where (which page) to turn for information about a topic.**
**The number or numbers after the topic tells to which page(s) to turn.**

Example:   Bighorn sheep, 89
Bison, 13, 23
Buffalo, 12-24

You can find information about bison on page 13 *and* on page 23.

3. On what page can you find information about bighorn sheep? _____

## PARTS OF SPEECH:   VERBS

**A regular verb adds ed to the past tense.**
**An irregular verb does not add ed to the past tense.**

Write **RV** for regular verb and **IV** for irregular verb.

4. a)  to walk - _____        c)  to wipe - _____

   b)  to eat - _____        d)  to do - _____

## SENTENCE COMBINING:

5. Bert slipped on a banana peel.
Bert grabbed onto the counter.

---

---

**DAY 172**

**CAPITALIZATION:**

**Do not capitalize names of diseases.** Examples: cold   flu   chicken pox

1.  will measles shots be given at milton hospital next tuesday?

**PUNCTUATION:**

2.  We cant be next Chris

_____

**PREFIXES/ROOTS/SUFFIXES:**
**A prefix is placed before a base or root word.** Example: **re**do
**A base word or root is a word or part of a word that contains meaning.**
Examples:   do, ped
**A suffix is an ending to a word.** Example: do**ing**, ped**al**
Match the prefix with its meaning.

3.  a) _____ sub          1.  again, backward
    b) _____ re           2.  under
    c) _____ un, il, non  3.  not

**PARTS OF SPEECH:   VERBS**

**A contraction is made up of two words.  A contraction has a letter or letters left out.  These letters are replaced by an apostrophe ( ' ).**
Write each contraction.

4.  a) I am - _____          c) will not - _____

    b) have not - _____          d) he is - _____

**SENTENCE COMBINING:**

5.  Jane swam across the pool.
    Jane yelled to her brother.

_____

_____

**CAPITALIZATION:**

1. was ms. marks a secretary for l. d. metro company?

**PUNCTUATION:**

**Place a comma after <u>asked</u> or <u>said</u> when someone is speaking. Place what the person says in quotation marks (" ").**

Poppa said, "Hi."

2. Mr Johns asked  Wheres the scouring pad

_____

**PARTS OF SPEECH:   NOUNS**

**By definition, common nouns do not name a specific person, place, or thing.  A *type* is still common and is not capitalized.**

|  | common noun | proper noun |
|---|---|---|
| Examples: | dog / poodle | Fifi (dog's name) |
|  | store / bakery | Mama's Pie Shop |

**Proper nouns name a specific person, place, or thing.  Capitalize them.**

Write a proper noun for each common noun.

3. a)  man - _____ b)  grocery store - _____

**TABLE OF CONTENTS:**

**A table of contents is placed at the beginning of a book.  It tells the title of each chapter and to which page you must turn to find that chapter.**

U. S. Presidents...................................4
Wives of Presidents............................22
U. S. Congress...................................45

4. To which page will you turn to find information about U. S. Presidents?_____

**SENTENCE COMBINING:**

5. Sammy jerked the reins.
His horse reared back.

_____

_____

**DAY 174**

## CAPITALIZATION:

**Capitalize the first word of each line of a poem.**

Capitalize this poem.

1. puddles are little lakes to wade in,

   not deep enough to be afraid in.

## PUNCTUATION:

Write the abbreviation.

2. a) United States - _____      c) Lane - _____

   b) East- _____              d) Doctor - _____

## PARTS OF SPEECH:   ADVERBS
**Adverbs can tell <u>when</u>, <u>where</u>, and <u>how</u>.**

3. A snail always crawls everywhere slowly.
   a) Which adverb tells <u>where</u> the snail crawls? _____
   b) Which adverb tells <u>how</u> the snail crawls? _____
   c) Which adverb tells <u>when</u> the snail crawls? _____

## PARTS OF SPEECH:   ADJECTIVES
<u>A</u>, <u>an</u>, and <u>the</u> are special adjectives called *articles*.
**Some adjectives tell *how many*.**    Examples:  **some** books
                                                  **four** balloons
**Some adjectives describe.**    Examples:  **tall green** grass
Circle *any* adjectives.

4. Two new blue hats are lying on a chair.

## SENTENCE COMBINING:

5. The White House is on Pennsylvania Avenue.
   The White House is in Washington, D. C.

   _____

   _____

## CAPITALIZATION:
Capitalize these two lines of a poem by William Thackeray.

1. first I saw the white bear, then I saw the black;

   then I saw the camel with a hump upon his back;

## PUNCTUATION:
Punctuate this outline.

2. I  Animal homes                    _____

     A  Mountain animals          _____

     B  Desert animals              _____

   II  Animal food                   _____

## PARTS OF SPEECH:  NOUNS
**Plural means more than one.  If a word ends in <u>sh</u>, <u>ch</u>, <u>s</u>, <u>x</u>, and <u>z</u>, add <u>es</u>.**
**If a word ends in a vowel + <u>y</u>, add <u>s</u>.**
**If a word ends in a consonant + <u>y</u>, change the <u>y</u> to <u>i</u> and add <u>es</u>.**
**Some words change form:    child – children.**
**Some words do not change:    moose – moose.**
Write the plural of each noun.

3.   a) fence - _____   c) cup - _____   e) mouse - _____

    b) brush - _____   d) ruby - _____   f) tray - _____

## PARTS OF SPEECH:  ADVERBS
**There are 7 adverbs often used to tell *to what extent*.**
**These are:  <u>not</u>, <u>so</u>, <u>very</u>, <u>too</u>, <u>quite</u>, <u>rather</u>, and <u>somewhat</u>.**

Write any adverb that tells <u>to what extent</u>.

4.  Jina walks _____ fast.

## SENTENCE COMBINING:

5.  Kari's toes are cold.
    Kari is wearing two pairs of socks.

    _____

    _____

**DAY 176**

**CAPITALIZATION:**

1.  we crossed hoover dam on the way to boulder city.

**PUNCTUATION:**

2.  Put Jonahs pants socks and shirts into the washer

_____

**PARTS OF SPEECH:   PRONOUNS**

Write the correct answer.

3.  _____ (Me and Zoey, Zoey and I) are ready.

**PREFIXES/ROOTS/SUFFIXES:**
   **Prefixes have meanings:**
            Examples:     sub = under
                          tri = three

4.  a)  A tricycle has _____ wheels.

    b)  A subway is a train that is _____ the ground.

**SENTENCE COMBINING:**

5.  Their dog is a cocker spaniel.
    Their dog wears sweaters in the winter.

_____

_____

_____

## CAPITALIZATION:

1.  is st. patrick's day* in march?

    *name of a special day

## PUNCTUATION:

Punctuate these titles.

2.  a) a nursery rhyme, Jack and Jill _____

    b) a book, Rosa _____

    c) a poem, Lemonade Stand _____

## DIFFICULT WORDS:

Write the correct answer.

3.  a) _____ ( They're, Their, There ) sitting in the middle row.

    b) _____ ( To, Too, Two ) girls left early.

    c) The cook doesn't have _____ ( any, no ) pepper.

## ALPHABETIZING:

Place these words in alphabetical order.

4.  brim     brook     cart     bend     draw

    (a) _____     (c) _____     (e) _____

    (b) _____     (d) _____

## SENTENCE COMBINING:

5.  Jacy's tent is new.
    Jacy will sleep in it tonight.

    _____

    _____

DAY 178

## CAPITALIZATION:

1. sally couldn't attend the founders' day rodeo* because she had mumps.
*name of a special event

## PUNCTUATION:
**Remember:  Place a comma after the name of a street when it is written in a sentence.  Place a comma between the city and state.  Do not place a comma between the state and the zip code.**

2. Pat lives at 20 Dree Drive Salinas California  93907

---

## PARTS OF SPEECH:   VERBS
*Tense means time.*  **Present tense means time now.**
Example:   The bells <u>ring</u> now.
**Past tense means that something already happened.**
Example:   Yesterday, the bells <u>rang</u>.
**Future tense means that something will happen.**
Example:   Tomorrow, the bells <u>will ring</u>.

Write the tense of each sentence.
3. a) _____ Linn rode her bike.    c) _____ Linn rides her bike.
   b) _____ Linn will ride her bike.

## PARTS OF SPEECH:   ADJECTIVES
**When you are comparing <u>2</u> things using a one-syllable adjective, use <u>er</u>.**
Example:  This vase is tall**er** than that one.
**When you are comparing <u>3 or more</u> things using a one-syllable adjective, use <u>est</u>.**      Example:  Lydia is tall**est** of the four girls.

Circle the correct adjective.
4. a) This ring is ( larger, largest ) than that ring.
   b) Of those six poles, I climbed the ( shorter, shortest ) one.

## SENTENCE COMBINING:

5. The winner is Susie.
   Susie is my neighbor.

---

---

## CAPITALIZATION:

Capitalize the name of a place of worship.  If only the *type* is given, capitalize only the type of a place of worship.

Examples:  **B**eth **A**mi **T**emple  -  a **J**ewish temple  (type)

**S**t. **J**ames **L**utheran **C**hurch  -  a **L**utheran church  (type)

1.  you will find northridge community church on dynamite road.

## PUNCTUATION:

2.  Lanas mom exclaimed  You did well

---

## SUBJECT/VERB:

**Remember:  A subject tells <u>who</u> or <u>what</u> the sentence is about.  A verb tells what <u>is</u> or what <u>happens</u> in a sentence.  If we can find a prepositional phrase in a sentence, we cross it out.  A word in a prepositional phrase will not be subject or verb.  (Some prepositions are *at, for, from, in, on, to,* and *with*.)**

Cross out any prepositional phrases.  Underline the subject once and the verb twice.

3.  Those flowers bloom in late spring.

## PARTS OF SPEECH:  VERBS

**Most verbs add <u>ed</u> to form the past tense.**

**Most verbs add <u>ed</u> if *has, have,* or *had* is used with them.**

Examples:  (to walk)  Ada walked home.  Ada *had walked* fast.

**Some verbs change form.  These are irregular verbs.**

Examples:  (to drink)  Scott drank water.  Scott *had drunk* water.

Select the correct verb.

4.  a)  Lexa ( drank, drinked ) two cups of water.
    b)  Their children ( rided, rode ) to a nearby farm.
    c)  Everyone had ( goed, gone ) home early.
    d)  We have ( buyed, bought ) some plums.

## SENTENCE COMBINING:

5.  Uncle Luke bought a bracelet for his wife.
    The bracelet is silver and has charms.

---

---

## CAPITALIZATION:

1.  jenny asked, "may i help to draw an american flag?"

## PUNCTUATION:

2.  Jims address is 22 Maple Street Rembert South Carolina   29128

_____

## SUBJECT/VERB:

**Remember:  A subject tells <u>who</u> or <u>what</u> the sentence is about.  A verb tells what <u>is</u> or what <u>happens</u> in a sentence.  If we can find a prepositional phrase in a sentence, we cross it out.  A word in a prepositional phrase will not be subject or verb. (Some prepositions are *at, for, from, in, on, to,* and *with*.)**

Example:   A <u>box</u> ~~of cereal~~ <u><u>fell</u></u> ~~from a shelf~~.

Cross out any prepositional phrases.  Underline the subject once and the verb twice.

3.  Her aunt from Florida arrived at the airport.

## PARTS OF A BOOK:   INDEX

**An index is located at the end of a book.  It helps you find the exact page or pages where information can be found.**

```
INDEX
     bats, 132
     birds, 87-90
        crows,  88-90
        robins,  90
     cats, 33-37
```

4.  On what pages will you find information about cats?  _____

## SENTENCE COMBINING:

5.  Micah was sick.
    Micah wanted to go out to play.

_____

_____

# Ideas and Suggestions for Effective Teaching

Please read each lesson's ideas and suggestions *before* beginning to discuss the lesson. Do each lesson *with* your students. Make copies of each lesson or purchase workbooks for each student. (Making a transparency will enhance learning.) In sentence #1, always discuss words that should be capitalized <u>and</u> why! Do likewise for punctuation used in sentence #2.

Keep in mind that new brain research reinforces the idea of relating new information to that which students already know. Be sure to use examples from your students' daily lives, their experiences, familiar places, etc. Be creative! Use your own ideas, too!

The beginning lessons will not require as much time. Look at the first 10 days of capitalization to get an idea as to how this text introduces, reviews, and spirals. Discuss all parts of each lesson. If you encounter a part of a lesson that you think is too difficult for your students, adapt it, or replace it.

If a number has been skipped in the following notes (for example, #3 in DAY 2), it signifies that no further instruction or comment is needed regarding that concept.

**DAY 1:**    **1.** You may want students to simply place a capital letter above the word that needs to be capitalized. Choose a method that meets your students' needs and coincides with your teaching style.    **2.** A line has been provided for students to write the phrase or sentence, if you choose for them to do so. Practice making an appropriate period.    **3.** If you think that the words are too easy, replace them.    **4.** In all sentence combining experiences, discuss and write various ways to express the two or three thoughts presented. Students can learn from both you *and* from their peers.

**DAY 2:**    **1.** You may wish to relate back to DAY 1, # 1 note. Having students write their name with middle initial is ideal. (You may wish to purchase white boards for each student to use. Students love writing on them, AND they help to make learning more personal and meaningful. See **www.easygrammar.com** for ordering.)    **2.** Practice making an appropriate question mark.    **4.** See DAY 1 note.

**DAY 3:**    **1.** The teachable moment may lead you to discuss the names of the days of the week.    **2.** See DAY 2 note.    **4.** See DAY 1 note. Also, you may wish to relate that no comma is used when two items are joined by a conjunction: *and, but, or.*

**DAY 4:**    **1.** You may wish to ask students in what grade they learned this rule. This serves to relate back to former knowledge.    **2.** Practicing with parents' or friends' names is helpful.
**4.** See DAY 1 and DAY 3 notes. You may wish to ask about whom we are talking in the sentence combining. This reinforces subject in #3 AND serves to pre-teach compound subject, which appears later in the text.

**DAY 5:**    **2.** Relate back to yesterday's lesson.    **3.** We have the same sentence as DAY 4. Review subject and then discuss what Sam does. You may want to begin having students place a line under the subject and two lines under the verb. (You may prefer for students to simply underline the verb twice rather than writing it on the line and then underlining it. Again, adapt your instruction to your students' needs and your teaching style.)    **4.** See DAY 1 note.

**DAY 6:**    **2.** See DAY 2 note.    **4.** See DAY 1 note.

**DAY 7:**   **2.** Practice making an appropriate exclamation mark (also called exclamation point). **3.** You may also want to discuss the subject. You may want to have students underline the subject once and the verb twice.   **4.** In all sentence combinings, discuss and write various ways to express the two or three thoughts presented. This helps students see how they can move away from short, choppy sentences.

**DAY 8:**   **1.** You may wish to discuss all of the months. (If you are using white boards, you may wish to ask students to write their birthday month [being sure to capitalize it]. This process enhances learning.) **3.** You will encounter these concepts throughout the text. You may want to discuss other suffixes that could be added *to talk*, e.g., *er, ed.*   **4.** See DAY 7 note.

**DAY 9:**   **2.** Be sure to discuss that Miss does not require a period. Ascertain that students are making appropriate question marks.   **4.** See DAY 7 note.

**DAY 10:**   **1.** Solicit examples from students. (White boards are helpful here.)   **4.** See DAY 7 note.

**DAY 11:**   **1.** *Family* is not capitalized here. You may want to point out that if their family's last name appears, capitalize the last name but not the word *family*.   **2.** See DAY 7 note.
**4.** See DAY 7 note. Also, you are introducing a compound verb as a sentence-combining possibility. You need not call it such, but be sure to point out that the subject *did* more than one thing. Also, note that a higher-level sentence structure using *as* has been provided as a possibility. You may introduce such a construction, decide to wait until later to introduce it, or choose to ignore it.

**DAY 12:**   **2.** You may choose to practice with the present date.   **3.** See DAY 1 note.
**4.** See DAY 7 note. Also, note that a higher-level sentence structure using *although* has been provided as a possibility. You may introduce such a construction, decide to wait until later to introduce it, or choose to ignore it.

**DAY 13:**   **1.** Solicit examples from students. (White boards are helpful here.)   **2.** Continue doing all lessons orally, soliciting both punctuation and reasons for use.   **4.** See DAY 11 note.

**DAY 14:**   **1.** As part of the teachable moment, I'd recommend that you have a large map of the United States on your wall. Ask students to find the state of Texas; then, ask students to find Austin. Where are Texas and Austin in relation to where they live? (I realize that some teachers may believe that this interferes with teaching language concepts. I have found that it enhances learning. However, do that which is best for your students and your teaching style.)   **2.** See DAY 13 note. Spend time on examples.

**DAY 15:**   **1.** Be sure to discuss titles with names, asking students for personal examples. (If using white boards, ascertain that students are capitalizing both the title and the name. Asking students to share their examples with a peer helps to reinforce the rule and serves as a check for proper capitalization.)   **3.** The verb will be discussed on DAY 16.   **4.** We are showing students the idea of cause and effect.

**DAY 16:**   **1.** Review titles with names using students' examples before discussing the sentence.   **2.** Solicit students' examples. (White boards are ideal here.)   **3.** See DAY 7 note. **4.** See DAY 7 note.

**DAY 17:**   **3.** Spend time helping students make appropriate apostrophes. Ascertain that they are placing the apostrophe where the letter has been deleted. **4.** See DAY 15 note.

182

**DAY 18:**    **2.** Spend time helping students make appropriate apostrophes. Ascertain that they are placing the apostrophe where the letter or letters have been omitted. **3.** You may want to discuss other suffixes that could be added. **4.** See DAY 7 note.

**DAY 19:**    **1.** Be sure to discuss why *Grandpa* should be capitalized. **2.** Solicit examples. You may want to use a map. **3.** See DAY 17 note. **4.** See DAY 4 note.

**DAY 20:**    **1.** Discuss various holidays. **2.** You may want to use your U. S. map. **3.** Solicit other examples. **4.** See DAY 7 note.

**DAY 21:**    **1.** You may want to discuss that foods are not capitalized. **2.** Be sure to discuss that Miss does not require a period. **4.** See DAY 7 note.

**DAY 22:**    **1.** Solicit students' examples. (White-board use is encouraged.) **3.** See DAY 1 note. **4.** See DAY 4 note.

**DAY 23:**    **1.** Review capitalizing names of streets, etc. **4.** See DAY 7 note. Also, note that a higher-level sentence structure using *when* has been provided as a possibility. You may introduce such a construction, decide to wait until later to introduce it, or choose to ignore it.

**DAY 24:**    **3.** Solicit other examples. **4.** See DAY 11 note.

**DAY 25:**    **2.** Check to see if students are making commas properly. **4.** See DAY 4 note.

**DAY 26:**    **2.** Review the rule for introductory words from yesterday's lesson. **3.** Adjectives are introduced throughout the text. (You may want students to draw an arrow from the adjective to the word it modifies.) **4.** See DAY 7 note.

**DAY 27:**    **3.** Students will be asked to identify the verb in the ensuing lesson. **4.** See DAY 7 note.

**DAY 28:**    **2.** Continue to ascertain that apostrophes and other types of punctuation are formed correctly. Check students' placement of the apostrophe in *isn't*. **4.** You may want to relate that no comma is used when two items are joined by the conjunctions: *and, but, or.* (Also, in the *teachable moment*, you may want to point out that *too* placed at the end of a sentence, as in the second sentence-combining sentence, is preceded by a comma. This is applicable to *also* as well.)

**DAY 29:**    **1.** Solicit examples of different local bodies of water and specific names. (White-board use is encouraged.) **2.** In good writing, the abbreviation for a month is not used within a sentence. However, it has been placed here for practice. **4.** See DAY 23 note.

**DAY 30:**    **1.** It is helpful for students to see a geographic place on a map. Reinforce capitalizing the name of a state. **3.** Solicit other examples of antonyms. **4.** See DAY 7 note.

**DAY 31:**    **1.** See DAY 30 note. **4.** See DAY 7 note.

**DAY 32:**    **3.** You may want to ask students to draw an arrow from *paper* to *bag.* **4.** See DAY 23 note.

**DAY 33:** **2.** You may want to review use of a comma after introductory words. **3.** Continue to check apostrophe formation and location. **4.** See DAY 7 note. Also discuss items in a series and placement of commas.

**DAY 34:** **2.** Have students write their names and something they *own*. (White-board use is ideal here.) Be sure to share that it doesn't matter if the student owns one item or many items. The placement of the apostrophe deals with singular or plural ownership, not number of items owned. **4.** See DAY 4 note. Showing students a neither/nor construction is optional.

**DAY 35:** **1.** Solicit local examples including names of hills, if possible. **2.** Review of yesterday's lesson is suggested. **3.** Solicit other examples. **4.** See DAY 7 note.

**DAY 36:** **4.** Point out that *but* may also be used.

**DAY 37:** **1.** You may want students to write the name of their school. Also, solicit names of former and/or neighboring schools. **2.** The second example should help children see that inanimate objects can *own* something. **3.** You may want students to determine the subject, also. Using one line to underline the subject and two lines under the verb is suggested.

**DAY 38:** **4.** This is a cause-effect construction. Although a sentence beginning with *because* in an adverbial clause is provided in the answer key, sharing it is optional.

**DAY 39:** **1.** Review the idea that the name of a family is capitalized but not the word *family.* **3.** You may want students to draw an arrow from *old* and *rusty* to *nail* to show that they modify *nail.* **4.** See DAY 7 note.

**DAY 40:** **4.** Stress that the other person, *Anna*, should be placed before *me*. **4.** Also see DAY 7 note.

**DAY 41:** **2.** Guide students to see that an apostrophe should be placed after the second <u>t</u> and before the final <u>s</u> in the name. **3.** You may want to clap out syllables in students' names. Personalizing learning enhances it. **4.** Also see DAY 7 note.

**DAY 42:** **2.** Although this rule is introduced formally here, you have been pre-teaching it in several sentence-combining examples. **4.** Also see DAY 7 note.

**DAY 43:** **2.** The rule for three items in a series was encountered and discussed in a former sentence combining. It is formally introduced here. **4.** Also see DAY 7 note.

**DAY 44:** **4.** This is reinforcement of the rule for items in a series from yesterday's lesson. **4.** See DAY 7 note.

**DAY 45:** **2.** Review the rules for possessive nouns. **4.** Compound verb construction can be used. Using *when* in a subordinate clause is also acceptable. Also see DAY 7 note.

**DAY 46:** **1.** Local examples are excellent. (White-board use helps to ensure that students are capitalizing examples properly.) **4.** This is ideal for forming a compound sentence using *but.* Emphasize that if the conjunction joins two complete sentences (a compound sentence), a comma is placed after the word before the conjunction. You may want to share other sentences using conjunctions in compound sentences. *Although* placed in front of *Jack's* may also be used.

**DAY 47:**    **2.**  Using a comma with a noun of direct address is introduced here.    **4.**  When using *I* and another person's name, place the other person's name first.  Guide students in subject-verb agreement to see that a compound subject necessitates the use of the verb *want*. Also see DAY 7 note.

**DAY 48:**    **3.**  You may want to discuss that one line indicates that *Mike* is the subject of the sentence.  Two underlines indicate that *paints* is the verb.    **4.**  See DAY 7 note.

**DAY 49:**    **1.**  Sports teams fall under the heading of organizations.    **3.**  You may want students to underline *Pam* (subject) once and *plays* (verb) twice.  Stress that the adverb tells *how* Pam plays.  You may want students to draw an arrow from *quietly* to *plays*.    **4.**  See DAY 7 note.

**DAY 50:**    **1.**  Students should learn rules for not capitalizing certain categories of words. **2.**  Guide students to see that *Brad* is a noun of direct address.    **4.**  See DAY 7 note.

**For DAYS 51-180, the DAY 7 cross reference no longer appears in #4.  You are encouraged, however, to continue to discuss and write various ways to express the two or three thoughts presented.  By now you are probably already aware that sentence combining helps students move away from writing short, choppy sentences.**

**DAY 51:**    **2.**  Be sure that students understand that they do not place a comma after the last item when three or more items are given in a series.    **3.**  You may want to instruct students to draw an arrow from *red* and *juicy* to *apples* to signify that they modify that noun.

**DAY 52:**    **1.**  This is the first time a one-word title is addressed.  Ask students for other examples.  Point out that we underline book titles.    **4.**  The subject becomes *foods*; therefore, the verb changes to *are*.  Also, no comma is used with two items.

**DAY 53:**    **1.**  The examples are very important.  Note that only the first word in the second example is capitalized.    **2.**  This should reinforce the teaching of #1.    **4.**  You may also wish to show students the neither-nor construction.

**DAY 54:**    **1.**  You may want to discuss that *Dear Ann,* is called the greeting of a letter and that *I miss you.* is referred to as the body or message.    **2.**  Guide students in understanding that someone is talking to *Tony*.    **4.**  A compound verb is reinforced here.  You may want to share the construction for using *when*.

**DAY 55:**    **4.**  Guide students to understand that *are* is used with a compound subject.

**DAY 56:**    **2.**  You may want to ask *what* belongs to Jill in ascertaining that students use singular possessive.    **3.**  This serves to introduce students to dictionary entries and abbreviations for parts of speech.    **4.**  This reintroduces students to using a conjunction in a compound sentence.  Students need to be reminded that the part of the sentence before and after *but* can each stand alone as a sentence. Therefore, a comma must be placed after the word that precedes the conjunction. This is another place where a complex sentence beginning with a dependent clause that starts with *although* may be used. You may choose not to share this construction.

**DAY 57:**   **3.** This is an introduction to subject-verb agreement.   **4.** See DAY 11 note.

**DAY 58:**   **4.** This is an introduction to a compound indirect object. Students do not need to know the technical name.

**DAY 59:**   **1.** Two-word titles are introduced here. Solicit examples from students. Point out that <u>The Farm</u> is underlined because it is the title of a book. Such pre-teaching serves to enhance later learning.   **3.** Pronouns listed are nominative pronouns used as subject (or predicate nominative, a concept that will not be introduced at this level).

**DAY 60:**   **3.** If you deem the list too easy, change it.   **4.** If the word *yesterday* is placed at the beginning of a sentence, it is usually followed by a comma. If it occurs at the end, no comma is used.

**DAY 61:**   **2.** You may want to review the rule that if two descriptive adjectives are side by side and one is a color, do not use a comma between them.   **3.** You may want to have students underline the subject once and the verb twice <u>and</u> draw an arrow from the adverb to the verb to show that the adverb helps to explain the verb.

**DAY 62:**   **1.** *Aunt* is not part of a title here.   **4.** This is another example of items in a series as a compound subject.

**DAY 63:**   **2.** Review that *Dear Jay,* is referred to as the greeting of the letter.   **3.** You will note that the definition of a phrase (a group of words) appears throughout the text. This helps students prepare for the concept of a prepositional phrase.   **4.** See DAY 56 note.

**DAY 64:**   **3.** Students will encounter the verb of this sentence in the next lesson.   **4.** See DAY 56 note.

**DAY 65:**   **1.** This reintroduces the concept of capitalizing only the first word in the closing of any letter.

**DAY 66:**   **3.** This lesson refers only to the past tense of regular verbs; irregular verbs will be introduced later.

**DAY 67:**   **1.** Only postal codes have been introduced here. Remind students that no period is used with a postal code. (After completing the first sentence, you may wish to discuss the house address and street address [15 Bell Street], the city [Reno], and the state [NV]. Point out that when an address is written within a sentence, a comma is placed after the street address, and one is placed between city and state. However, no comma is placed between the state and zip code. In doing so, you will be pre-teaching a concept that will be taught later in the text.)

**DAY 68:**   **2.** The use of underlining for book titles and quotation marks for short stories is introduced. Ascertain that students make quotation marks well.

**DAY 69:** **1.** You may want to discuss friendly letter parts: greeting, message/body, closing, and signature. The heading of a friendly letter will be introduced later. **2.** Make sure that students place quotation marks appropriately as well as form them well. **4.** Students will use subject-verb agreement here. Discuss that when the subject becomes plural, s is not added to the verb.

**DAY 70:** **4.** The use of *both-and* is common in our language. Often, it is used for emphasis.

**DAY 71:** **1.** Discussing parts of a letter after completion is advised. See DAY 69 note. **3.** The idea of a phrase is introduced within the context of a prepositional phrase. **4.** See DAY 23 note.

**DAY 72:** **1.** The possessive can refer to more than owning, i.e., sharing or belonging. **4.** This is an introduction to a sequence of events. Help students to perceive that this may be written in more than one way.

**DAY 73:** **1.** You may want to solicit examples of languages from students. **3.** You may want students to clap sounds of polysyllabic words. **4.** The compound subject requires the helping verb *have* for subject-verb agreement.

**DAY 74:** **1.** Students are introduced to capitalizing the first word of a direct quotation. **2.** Building on #1, students are introduced to the idea of placing someone's exact words in quotation marks. Practice making quotation marks. Guide students to see that the sentence should end with a question mark; place the quotation marks <u>after</u> the question mark. **3.** See DAY 61 note.

**DAY 75:** Before doing # 1 and #2, you may want to ask a simple question such as *Where do you live?* and have a student respond. Write the response on a transparency, using the student's name, *said*, a comma, and placing the exact words in quotation marks. Use other questions and responses. If students are using white boards, you may want to pair them. Have one student ask a simple question, and the other write a response, placing his or her name first, the word *said*, and a comma. Both students can work together on the response. Don't expect mastery at this point. **3.** You may want to reproduce a dictionary page so that students can see an example of guide words.

**DAY 76:** **2.** Review underlining and quotation marks before you discuss this sentence.

**DAY 77:** **2.** Also teach comma placement in the second example. **4.** This can be written as a simple sentence. It also can be written as a cause-effect sentence using *because*.

**DAY 78:** **1.** You will note that throughout the text, rules are repeated to help students learn. **4.** Subject-verb agreement is important here.

**DAY 79:** **4.** With items in a series, be sure students place a comma after the word preceding the conjunction.

**DAY 80:** **3.** It is important for students to understand that prefixes, roots, and suffixes give meaning to words.

**DAY 81:** **3.** See DAY 75 note. **4.** See DAY 11 note.

**DAY 82:**   **3.** You may want to discuss past tense.

**DAY 83:**   **4.** See DAY 11 note.

**DAY 84:**   **1.** Discuss various land formations and solicit examples of specific names.

**DAY 85:**   **4.** See DAY 7 note.

**DAY 86:**   **4.**  This can be written as cause-effect.

**DAY 87:**   **4.** See DAY 7 note.

**DAY 88:**   **2.** An address within a sentence is presented here.  Be sure that students understand where to place commas.

**DAY 89:**   **2.** Guide students to see how singular and plural possessives are formed.

**DAY 90:**   **2.** After completing punctuation, discuss the names for the various friendly-letter parts.   **3.** Objective pronouns are introduced here.   **4.** Note that the answer key suggests several ways of combining this sentence.


**You will note that DAYS 1-90 have just four components.  DAYS 91-180 have five.**


**DAY 91:**   **2.** Use of a colon with time is introduced here.   **5.** Subject-verb agreement is important with a compound subject.

**DAY 92:**   **3.** Students will use an objective pronoun.   **5.** See DAY 91 note.

**DAY 93:**   **5.** Most students will use the singular possessive in writing this sentence.

**DAY 94:**   **3.** See DAY 61 note.

**DAY 95:**   **3.** See DAY 26 note.   **4.** Try to guide students to make the pronoun singular and male (*his*) for the antecedent, *Jay*.

**DAY 96:**   **3.** Double negatives are especially difficult for students whose family uses them. Your goal for those students is to change academic behavior.

**DAY 97:**   **3.** Drawing an arrow from the adjective to the noun it modifies is recommended.

**DAY 98:**   **3.** Ascertain that an appropriate apostrophe is made and that it appears where a letter or letters have been omitted.

**DAY 99:**   **2.** Be sure that the question mark is placed inside the end quotation marks.
**3.** See DAY 96 note.

188

**DAY 100:**   **3.** You may want to guide students to underline the subject once and the verb phrase, *will eat*, twice.  In asking students to draw a line from the adverb to the verb, help them to perceive that the adverb helps to explain the verb.  **4.** You may ask students to underline the subject once.

**DAY 101:**   **2.** Students will use the plural possessive because of the reference to more than one sister.

**DAY 102:**   **3.** In discussion, you may ask students what they will do this evening.  Have them respond in a complete sentence.  Technically, *shall* should be used with *I*.

**DAY 103:**   **1.** After capitalization has been completed, you may want to discuss letter parts.

**DAY 104:**   **2.** You may want to ask students to identify the other two parts of the friendly letter.  **3.** See DAY 96 note.

**DAY 105:**   **3.** Add words if you want to make alphabetizing more challenging.  **4.** You may want to ask students to draw arrows from each limiting adjective to the noun it modifies.  **5.** Students are being introduced to expository (informational) writing.

**DAY 106:**   **3.** Be sure to discuss students' answers  **4.** After completing this part, you may wish to sound out (clap) various names of those who work at your school:  secretary, principal, custodian, food service workers, etc.  **5.** Although this is a short combination, it denotes cause-effect.

**DAY 107:**   **5.** See DAY 105 note.

**DAY 108:**   **5.** See DAY 46, #4 note.

**DAY 109:**   **3.** See DAY 1 note.

**DAY 110:**   **3.** You may want to add that *will start* is future tense.  You may want to have students draw an arrow from *soon* to *will start* to show that the adverb helps to explain the verb.  **5.** See DAY 105 note.

**DAY 111:**   **5.** See DAY 105 note.

**DAY 112:**   **4.** You may want to expand this lesson with more examples.

**DAY 113:**   **1.** If you set this rule to movement with a jazzy tune, students usually learn it more quickly.  (I recommend movement and songs in the teaching-learning process.)  **4.** You may want to reteach these concepts, providing additional examples.  **5.** See DAY 105 note.

**DAY 114:**   **2.** You may want to review the rule about comma placement for city and state (with none between state and zip code) before beginning this part.  **4.** Asking students who could eat soup, a sandwich, *and* a salad for lunch may personalize this for them.  How many students would use *or* because they could not eat all three items? This personalizes the teaching.  **5.** For your information: *Glass music box* does not require a comma between the two adjectives because *music box* is seen as a separate entity.  Although most students have not mastered the comma-between-two-equal-adjectives rule, this information has been added for your understanding.

**DAY 115:** **1.** Your map may not include Bear Island. **3.** Continuing to draw arrows from the adjective to the noun or pronoun it modifies is helpful. **5.** See DAY 105 note.

**DAY 116:** **4.** If children have learned incorrect usage at home, it will be a challenge for you to change academic behavior. Repetition of correct usage helps to make that change.

**DAY 117:** **3.** This introduces the concept of deleting prepositional phrases as a means of determining subject and verb. (This process is continued in higher-level *Easy Grammar* texts.) **5.** See DAY 23, #4 note. *Because* may also be used.

**DAY 118:** **2.** You may want to have students write today's complete date. **3.** This builds upon yesterday's lesson.

**DAY 119:** **2.** You may want to review the concept of an interjection. Discuss that this is an exclamatory sentence. **3. Be sure to do the step-by-step process of finding and deleting prepositional phrases. Again, the subject and verb (and usually other concepts, i. e., direct objects, predicate nominatives will not be in a prepositional phrase. You are helping students to understand their language.** **5.** The correlative conjunctions, *both-and*, may be used here.

**DAY 120:** **1.** Discuss local events and write them to show capitalization. (Use of white boards is encouraged.) **2.** *Too* may also mean *overly*: *The pie is too sweet.* This meaning is not introduced in this text. **5.** This is a good place to discuss cause and effect.

**DAY 121:** **3.** After determining adjectives, you may want to find subject and verb (<u>He</u> <u>has</u>).

**DAY 122:** **2.** See DAY 119 note. **3.** Guide students to underline the subject once and the verb twice before determining if the verb shows action. In the second sentence, *are* is the verb. If students believe that *happy* may be part of it, show them *to happy*. Ask if we say: Today, I happy. Yesterday I happied. No! *Happy* is not part of the verb. **5.** Continue emphasizing that a comma is used in a compound sentence. Show students the sentence structure using *when Nan dropped her dime* at the end of the sentence. You may wish to show students the clause placed at the beginning—an iintroductory adverbial clause: *When Nan dropped her dime.*

**DAY 123:** **2.** See DAY 114 note. **3.** This is simply a review of subject and verb. You may want to guide students to see that *always* is an adverb telling when her sister flosses. (You may want to discuss flossing and good dental hygiene.)

**DAY 124:** **1.** After completing capitalization, you may want to discuss letter parts: greeting, message or body, closing, and signature. **3.** Although articles are limiting adjectives, they do modify. You may wish to continue to draw arrows. You will probably want to discuss that *an* is used before the word *open*. **4.** You may want to provide examples of other nouns that totally change to form the plural. **5.** Subject-verb agreement is reinforced here.

**DAY 125:** **4.** Compound pronoun usage is very important in speaking and writing. You may want students to say a friend's name and *I* and then complete a sentence. Saying it enhances mastery. **5.** This introduces the idea of a relative clause: *that his aunt and uncle gave him.* An appositive could also be introduced: *a gift from his aunt and uncle.*

190

**DAY 126:** **3.** Discuss examples of common and proper nouns that are meaningful to your students. **5.** See DAY 122 note, adapting the example to this sentence combining.

**DAY 127:** **3.** Subject-verb agreement is extremely important. Teach it carefully.
**4.** Possessive pronouns must agree in number and gender with an antecedent. Students do not need to know these terms now; however, students need to understand that *their* refers to more than one. **5.** This reinforces the lesson in #3.

**DAY 128:** **3.** You may want to review *to, too,* and *two* before completing this sentence.
**5.** See DAY 122 note, adapting the example to this sentence combining.

**DAY 129:** **3.** Have students practice reading correct usage aloud. This helps to reinforce it.

**DAY 130:** **1.** Before doing # 1, you may want to ask a simple question (*What is your favorite school subject?*) and have a student respond. Write the response using the student's name, *said*, a comma, and placing the exact words in quotation marks. If students are using white boards, you may want to pair them. Have one student ask a simple question, and the other write a response, placing the name first, the word *said*, and a comma. Both students can work together on the response. **3.** Objective pronouns are listed on the second line. You may want to point out the pairs of nominative/objective pronouns: *I/me, he/him, she/her, they/them, we/us,* and *who/whom.* (*It* and *you* are neutral and can be used both as objective and nominative pronouns.) **5.** See DAY 122 note, adapting the example to this sentence combining. *As* may be used.

**DAY 131:** **3.** After completing the instructions, you may want to solicit from students that the sentence type is a command. If you think students are ready, introduce the idea of (You) as the subject. (You) is stated as *you understood.* The concept is not formally introduced in this text.
**4.** After determining subject and verb, you may want to discuss that *brightly* is an adverb telling *how* the model smiled. **5.** See Day 105 note.

**DAY 132:** **3.** Ascertain that students draw a **straight** line to delete prepositional phrases.

**DAY 133:** **2.** Use of hyphens is introduced here. Having students write their own examples is suggested. **3.** Saying this sentence orally helps to change academic behavior of those who use it improperly. **4.** After determining subject and verb, you may also want to discuss that *well* is an adverb telling *how.* **5.** Note that a higher-level sentence structure using *although* works well here. You may use such a construction, decide to wait until later to introduce it, or choose to ignore it.

**DAY 134:** **2.** Reviewing use of underlining and quotation marks is a good idea before beginning this lesson. **3.** This introduces that a root may be a word that can stand alone or part of a word. You may also want to discuss that *vis* is a root that means *sight* and draw from students the meaning of the word *vision.* **5.** This sentence combining requires a cause-effect relationship.

**DAY 135:** **1.** See DAY 124 note. **4.** See DAY 131, #3 note.

**DAY 136:** **1.** You may have to remind students that Mexico is the name of a country.
**3.** Once again, be sure that students use a straight line through a prepositional phrase. (If students become careless and only delete the *me* in *meadow*, for example, they may think

that *meadow* still remains as an option for subject.)

**DAY 137:**   **3.** Reinforce that *I*, not *me*, must be used.   **4.** Students should be gaining an understanding of adding meaning through the use of prefixes and suffixes.

**DAY 138:**   **1.** To reinforce underlining book titles, you may want to discuss that <u>Charlotte's Web</u> is a book   **4.** Use many examples in discussing *your* and *you're*.   **5.** The sentences do not reflect if the taxi driver slowed because the lady crossed the street or to allow the lady to cross the street.  This gives much latitude in students' sentence composition.

**DAY 139:**   **1.** See DAY 113 note.  Analyze the title word for word.   **3.** You may want to discuss that the roots *scrib* and *script* have to do with writing:  Examples:  scribe, scripture, prescription   **4.** After identifying subject and verb, you may want to discuss that *softly* tells *how* the cat purred.  Have students draw an arrow from *softly* to *purred* to show that the word helps to explain the verb.

**DAY 140:**   **1.** See DAY 113 note.  Using the rule, analyze the title carefully.   **3.** You may want to discuss that the table of contents is located in the front of a book or magazine.   **4.** After completing the task, you may want to ask if students can find a special adjective called an *article* in the sentence (<u>a</u>).  Be sure to discuss the other two articles as well.   **5. If at any time you think that sentence-combining sentences are too difficult, you may choose to delete one of them.**

**DAY 141:**   **5.** See DAY 56, #4 note.

**DAY 142:**   **1.** See DAY 124 note.   **3.** The letter combination <u>iy</u> has been omitted because no English words end in <u>iy</u>.   **4.** You may want to refer to *mom* and *I* as the antecedent simply to introduce the term.   **5.** When referring to people, *who*—not *that*—should be used to begin a relative clause.

**DAY 143:**   **1.** You may want to discuss and locate Niagara Falls.   **3.** The prepositional approach will help students refrain from thinking that *Grandma* arrived.   **5.** See DAY 142 note.

**DAY 144:**   **1.** Also solicit names of other geographic places.   **3.** You may want to ask what *repainting* means.  Has their family ever repainted something?  Giving personal meaning enhances learning.   **5.** This reintroduces students to using a conjunction in a compound sentence.  Remind students that the part of the sentence before <u>and</u> after *but* can stand alone as a sentence.  Therefore, a comma is needed.

**DAY 145:**   **2.** The word *these* is used to imply more than one.   **4.** The rules for *vowel + y* and *consonant + y* are very important.  Teach them carefully.   **5.** Discuss use of *apostrophe + s* when using *Karn's*.

**DAY 146:**   **1.** *American* is the only reference to a proper adjective in this text.  Use other examples if you think your students will understand.   **3.** You may also want to ask students to underline the subject *Janice* once.   **4.** You may wish to have students draw an arrow from each article to the noun it modifies (The/group; an/inn; a/village).   **5.** See DAY 133 note.

**DAY 147:**   **1.** This is a simple introduction to an outline.  Capitalizing Roman numerals is not introduced.  **2.** This is an introduction to placing a comma after person speaking + verb (said). Students usually do well following patterns if they are presented consistently.  **5.** Emphasis is placed on writing items in a series. Also, subject-verb agreement is important.

**DAY 148:**  **1.** You may want to discuss this special day.  **2.** Guide students to place a comma after *asked*.  **3.** This is an introduction to comparison (degree) of adjectives. Only one-syllable words are addressed in this text.  **4.** You may want to guide students to determine subject and verb. Here we have a two-word verb referred to as a verb phrase. (You may want to relate it back to a phrase meaning more than one word.) Do students remember what tense *will eat* is? (Even if they don't recall, your sharing leads towards mastery.)

**DAY 149:**  **1.** See DAY 124 rule.  **2.** If you want to include a math lesson, determine how old David's dad is now.  **5.** Students are practicing compound-verb composition here.

**DAY 150:**  **1.** See DAY 113 note.  **4.** You may wish to reteach *their, there,* and *they're* before completing this lesson.  **5.** This is a sequence of events.

**DAY 151:**  **4.** You may wish to add that nouns also name ideas such as *freedom* and *love*. Abstract nouns have not been included in this text.  **5.** Subject-verb agreement is important.

**DAY 152:**  **3.** You may want students to draw arrows from adjectives to the nouns (Some, small, red/cherries; a, tin/bucket).  **4.** Asking students to underline *Jack* as the subject is suggested.

**DAY 153:**  **2.** After completing this lesson, you may want to review that the first word after each section is capitalized. Capitalization of Roman numerals has not been discussed.

**DAY 154:**  **1.** Underlining plays and movies and using quotation marks for poems and songs have been added. Be sure to ask for many examples.  (White-board use is encouraged.)

**DAY 155:**  **3.** The terms—*declarative, interrogative, imperative,* and *exclamatory*—are introduced here.  **4.** Teach students that *I, he, she, we, they, who, you,* and *it* can be used as the subject of a sentence. Therefore, *Ann* has to be replaced by *she*. (This may be difficult for students who have always used *her*.)

**DAY 156:**  **3.** You may want students to determine subject and verb phrase, also. Ask what tense *will walk* is. This reinforces the concept of future tense.  **5.** Guide students to see that other possibilities besides a compound sentence may be used.

**DAY 157:**  **1.** Placement of the speaker after the quotation is introduced. Mastery is not expected.  **4.** You may want students to underline the verb, *made*, twice.

**DAY 158:**  **1.** Do these together with students. Using the rule, analyze each title, word for word.  **3.** Saying the correct usage helps to reinforce correct speaking. **4.** Regular and irregular verbs are introduced here. More examples may be helpful.  **5.** See DAY 11, #4 note.

**DAY 159:**  **3.** Regular and irregular verbs are reintroduced here.

**DAY 160:**  **3.** You may want to underline the subject once and the verb twice after deleting prepositional phrases (<u>Jana</u> <u>went</u>).  **4.** If you have been reinforcing parts of a friendly letter, only the heading is new here.  Discuss in detail the components of a heading.  You may want to have students write a letter at the completion of DAY 160.  (If privacy is an issue, allow them to create an address.)

**DAY 161:**   **1.** See DAY 157 note.   **2.** After completing punctuation of the letter, you may want to discuss components of a heading again.   **3.** These are the most common; there are others. **4.** You may want to ask to what the word *your* refers.  Using the word, antecedent, again lays the groundwork for later learning.

**DAY 162:**   **1.** See DAY 158 note.   **4.** You may want students to underline the verb, *move*, also.  **5.** See DAY 11, #4 note.

**DAY 163:**   **2.** Review all lines of a heading.

**DAY 164:**   **3.** Although it's not given as a direction, you may ask students to delete the prepositional phrase, *to his friend*.

**DAY 165:**   **1.** You may wish to discuss the names of other continents.   **2.** You may need to point out that *St.* can be the abbreviation for *street* or *saint*.   **4.** This is an important concept for speaking and writing properly.  You may want students to share some activity, such as playing soccer, that they do well.  This reinforces the use of *well* with an action verb.

**DAY 166:**   **1.** After completing capitalization, you may want to discuss the parts of a heading. **4.** You may want to have students draw an arrow from each adjective to the noun it modifies. This will show students that an adjective does not have to precede a noun.  This sets the course for learning about predicate adjectives later.

**DAY 167**   **3.** You may want to have students delete the prepositional phrase, *on the pond,* and underline the verb, *swim*, twice.  **4.** Use clapping or any other technique to help students understand this concept.

**DAY 168:**   **4.** It is important for students to understand that I, he, she, we, they, who, you, and it are used as the subject.  (That is why *My friend and me….* is incorrect.)

**DAY 169:**   **2.** This "hint" in punctuating titles appears in higher-level *Easy Grammar* texts. However, it is worth introducing here.  **3.** To reinforce prior learning, refer to *will go* as a verb phrase.   **4.** You may want to help students determine that the subject of this imperative sentence is (You)—*You* understood.  The verb is *take*.  **5.** See DAY 46, #4 note.

**DAY 170:**   **1.** To help students determine if *the* should be capitalized as part of the event's title, ask them to visualize what a sign at the event may say. Usually the sign will not include *the.*

**DAY 171:**   **4.** You may want to review examples of regular and irregular verbs.  **5.** See DAY 7, #4 note.

**DAY 172:**   **1.** If students discuss a disease such as German measles or Parkinson's disease, explain why these words are capitalized.

194

**DAY 173:** **3.** You may want to give students various examples of types as common nouns.

**DAY 174:** **3.** You may want students to underline the subject, *snail,* and place two lines under the verb, *crawls,* before determining adverbs. Drawing arrows from the adverbs to the verb is also suggested. **4.** Drawing arrows from the adjectives to the nouns is also recommended: Two, new, blue/hats; a/chair.

**DAY 175:** **2.** You may want to review punctuating outlines. **4.** These are common adverbs that tell *to what extent*; there are others. You may want to guide students to see that *fast* is also an adverb. It tells *how* Tammi walks.

**DAY 176:** **3.** You may want to discuss why *Me and Zoey* is incorrect.

**DAY 177:** **2.** Reviewing the rules for punctuation of titles is suggested. **3.** Reviewing the words in parts *a* and *b* is recommended. You may want to discuss why *any* in part *c* is correct. Reading this sentence orally helps to reinforce correct usage.

**DAY 178:** **5.** You may want to teach a simple lesson about appositives so that students can more readily understand placement of both the appositive and commas.

**DAY 179:** **1.** The rule for capitalizing places of worship has already been covered with capitalization of buildings. The capitalization of a faith is new and placed here to simply introduce a concept that students will learn later. **4.** This introduces students to using the helping verbs, *has, have,* and *had,* with an irregular verb. Mastery is not expected.

**DAY 180:** **1.** The proper adjective, *American,* appears here to reintroduce capitalization of adjectives that are based on a proper noun.

ശശശശശഹഹഹഹ

**ANSWERS:**

**AMV/RA** = Answers May Vary/Representative Answer(s)
   **Note:** Other ways of combining sentences may be used.

**DAY 1:** 1. Nancy   2. I like you.   3. a) boy  b) dog  c) girl   4. AMV/RA: That ball is round and green.  That green ball is round.  That round ball is green.

**DAY 2:** 1. Bob H. Smith   2. Are you going?   3. kite   4. AMV/RA: My red shirt is torn.  My torn shirt is red.

**DAY 3:** 1. Tuesday   2. Is that your pen?   3. AMV/RA: call, ball, wall
4. AMV/RA: Bob likes peanut butter and honey.  Bob likes honey and peanut butter.  Bob likes both peanut butter and honey.

**DAY 4:** 1. Her   2. Mr. Jones   3. Sam   4. AMV/RA: Jill and Ken jumped up. Ken and Jill jumped up.  Both Jill and Ken jumped up

**DAY 5:** 1. His, Joe   2. Mrs. Smith   3. eats   4. AMV/RA: His new car is blue.  His blue car is new.

**DAY 6:** 1. Tom, I   2. May I go?   3. friend   4. AMV/RA: His black hair is shiny.  His shiny hair is black.  His hair is black and shiny.

**DAY 7:** 1. May, I, Monday   2. We won!   3. chews   4. AMV/RA: Peter ate a red apple.  The apple that Peter ate was red.

**DAY 8:** 1. April   2. Mr. and Mrs. Little   3. wishing   4. AMV/RA: Tammy threw a large ball.  The ball that Tammy threw is large.

**DAY 9:** 1. Sunday, February 10   2. Did Miss Barnes leave?   3. mall
4. AMV/RA: Josh ran fast to the store.

**DAY 10:** 1. AMV/RA: Buffalo, Cornville   2. Mr. and Mrs. Simms are here today.   3. sail   4. AMV/RA: Kim hit the ball hard.

**DAY 11:** 1. My, I, America   2. You are the winner!   3. park   4. AMV/RA: The baby laughed and threw a rattle.  The baby threw a rattle and laughed.  As the baby laughed, he threw his rattle.

**DAY 12:** 1. Their, Mexico   2. My birthday is Thursday, March 12.   3. a) list b) sock  c) trip   4. AMV/RA: Some people like to climb that high hill. Although the hill is high, some people like to climb it.

**DAY 13:** 1. AMV/RA: Central, Avenue, Roe, Street   2. Does school start on Monday, September 7?   3. dad   4. AMV/RA: The dog barked and chased us. The barking dog chased us.

**DAY 14**:  1.  They, Austin, Texas  2.  Is Dr. Evans nice?  3.  by  4.  AMV/RA: Barry's paper is lying on the floor.

**DAY 15**:  1.  The, Dr., Lipton  2.  12 Elm St.  3.  lizard  4.  AMV/RA: The baby cried because he (she) was hungry.  The hungry baby cried.

**DAY 16**:  1.  Today, Aunt, Jane  2.  Becky was born October 21, 1989.
3.  crawled  4.  AMV/RA: The red dish is cracked.  The cracked dish is red.

**DAY 17**:  1.  Friday, July 10  2.  Sunday, May 10  3.  isn't  4.  AMV/RA: Jack drank a glass of water because he was thirsty.

**DAY 18**:  1.  On, Tuesday, I, Nevada  2.  Isn't Jenny here?  3.  pushed
4.  AMV/RA:  Cindy has a new purple wagon.

**DAY 19**:  1.  Linda, Grandpa, Wells  2.  Kingman, Arizona  3.  haven't
4.  AMV/RA:  Mary tickles her brother and sister.

**DAY 20**:  1.  I, Valentine's, Day  2.  Ken lives in Topeka, Kansas  3.  a) girls
b) cars  4.  AMV/RA:  A clown threw three balls up in the air.

**DAY 21**:  1.  Does, Thanksgiving  2.  Miss Sarah P. Kent  3.  a) thumbs
b) wishes  4.  AMV/RA:  His white kitten is a week old.  His week-old kitten is white.

**DAY 22**:  1.  They, Poppa's, Pizza  2.  Wow!  3.  a) egg  b) father  c) ham
4.  AMV/RA:  Tom and Sue walked home.

**DAY 23**:  1.  Her, Tulip, Avenue  2.  April 10, 2015  3.  pan  4.  AMV/RA: Paco yelled because he stubbed his toe.  Paco stubbed his toe and yelled. When Paco stubbed his toe, he yelled.

**DAY 24**:  1.  Is, Father's, Day, June  2.  Sunday, November 10  3.  fireman
4.  AMV/RA:  A tiny baby opened his eyes and waved his arms.  As the tiny baby opened his eyes, he waved his arms.

**DAY 25**:  1.  The, Pet, Palace  2.  No, I am not going.  3.  AMV/RA: road, lane, drive  4.  AMV/RA:  Brad and his sister went home.

**DAY 26**:  1.  Mr., Flogg, Aero, Airlines  2.  Yes, Mrs. Eller voted.  3.  tiny
4.  AMV/RA:  That frying pan is full of hot water.

**DAY 27**:  1.  In, March, I  2.  C-mt. A-st. B-ft.  3.  brother  4.  AMV/RA: Mary pulls her sister in a blue wagon.

**DAY 28**:   1.  Does, Mr., Sparks, Elm, Street    2.  Mrs. Argus isn't leaving today.
3.  runs    4.  AMV/RA:  We will eat hot dogs and beans for lunch.

**DAY 29**:   1.  Our, Skunk, Creek    2.  Yeah!  We're taking a Nov. vacation.
3.  a) bugs  b) ditches  c) eyelashes    4.  AMV/RA:  Jenny fell and scraped
her knee.  When Jenny fell, she scraped her knee.

**DAY 30**:   1.  My, Big, Clear, Lake, Wisconsin    2.  272 S. Central Avenue
3.  AMV/RA:  cold    4.  AMV/RA:  Their street is wide and paved.  Their paved
street is wide.

**DAY 31**:   1.  Mary, Pacific, Ocean    2.  1909 E. Flower Lane    3.  car, bikes
4.  AMV/RA:  The bear is eating berries and honey.

**DAY 32**:   1.  I, Dr., Fisk's    2.  Tampa, Florida    3.  paper    4.  AMV/RA:  Tate
raced his friends and won.  When Tate raced his friends, he won.

**DAY 33**:   1.  Her, Bell, Company    2.  Yes, Jane lives at 6003 N. Oak Trail.
3.  aren't    4.  AMV/RA:  Their horse likes carrots, apples, and hay.

**DAY 34**:   1.  You, Mississippi, River    2.  student's name + item    3.  show
4.  AMV/RA:  Ricky and Lucy can't go.  Neither Ricky nor Lucy can go.*
    *Although this is a difficult construction, it is worth introducing.

**DAY 35**:   1.  Have, Camelback, Mountain    2.  Pat's shells    3.  a) rugs
b) buses    4.  AMV/RA:  This rose with a long stem is pink.  This long-stemmed
rose* is pink.    For children who have heard the phrase, *long-stemmed rose*, this will not be
such a difficult construction.

**DAY 36**:   1.  We, Mt., Shasta    2.  Monday, August 27    3.  driveway
4.  AMV/RA:  My mom's friend drives slowly and carefully.

**DAY 37**:   1.  Next, I, Hilltop, School    2.  dog's    3.  sings    4.  AMV/RA:  This
yellow paper is torn.  This torn paper is yellow.

**DAY 38**:   1.  Does, Kent, Copper, Lane    2.  Dr. and Mrs. Potts were here in
Dec. for a week.    3.  AMV/RA:  small, tiny    4.  AMV/RA:  Kala is happy
because she has won a spelling bee.  Because Kala has won a spelling bee, she
is happy.

**DAY 39**:   1.  The, Harris, Briar, Park    2.  Yes, I'm glad you came.    3.  old,
rusty    4.  AMV/RA:  Lulu is in the band and in the chorus.  Lulu is in both band
and chorus.

**DAY 40**:   1.  Is, Easter, April    2.  D-Ln., B-E., A-yd., C-Mt.    3.  watch
4.  AMV/RA:  Paco gave Anna and me yo-yos.

**DAY 41**: 1. Her, Westway, Airlines 2. Scott's dad is a dentist.
3. AMV/RA: rug, friend 4. AMV/RA: Patty jumps rope nearly every day.

**DAY 42**: 1. She, Linnwood, Park, Tuesday 2. Their skates aren't blue and red. 3. AMV/RA: bat, rat, mat 4. AMV/RA: A white bunny hopped toward me.

**DAY 43**: 1. Tot, Toy, Store, Ohio 2. Nan ate fish, beans, and rice for dinner.
3. they're 4. AMV/RA: The green rug is smooth. The smooth rug is green.

**DAY 44**: 1. In, February, Dr., Lisper 2. No, today is not Friday, May 15.
3. beach 4. AMV/RA: Grandma swims, plays golf, and goes to college.

**DAY 45**: 1. Our, Rooster, Restaurant 2. Andy's 3. chair 4. AMV/RA:
When Tate fell down a step, he hurt his knee. Tate fell down a step and hurt his knee.

**DAY 46**: 1. Is, Hanover, Hospital, Pennsylvania 2. Their brother and sister went to Rutland, Vermont. 3. Yes 4. AMV/RA: Jack's mom wanted a turtle, but she bought a lizard. Although Jack's mom wanted a turtle, she bought a lizard.*

*This, perhaps, is a difficult construction for second graders. However, it is worth modeling.

**DAY 47**: 1. Has, Aunt, Betty, Rome 2. Barbara, aren't you ready?
3. a) churches b) tires c) dashes 4. AMV/RA: Jana and I want pets.

**DAY 48**: 1. In, August, Harper, Hospital 2. Yes, I'll take one. 3. paints
4. AMV/RA: The brown ground is soft and muddy. The ground is soft, muddy, and brown.

**DAY 49**: 1. We, Chicago, Cubs 2. Miss Ann K. Cline will drive. 3. quietly
4. AMV/RA: Our baseball team won!

**DAY 50**: 1. Next, I, Uncle, Todd 2. Brad, may Don and I come with you?
3. a) couldn't b) he's c) can't 4. AMV/RA: Ira will go to a museum tomorrow at 2:30 in the afternoon.

**DAY 51**: 1. We, Monday, June 2. We saw bears, monkeys, and lions at the zoo. 3. red, juicy 4. AMV/RA: The gift has silver paper and a blue bow. The gift has silver paper, but it has a blue bow.

**DAY 52**: 1. His, Bambi 2. dad's 3. jump 4. AMV/RA: His favorite foods are steak and cheese pizza. Steak and cheese pizza are his favorite foods.

**DAY 53**: 1. Dear, Billy 2. Dear Paul, 3. asking 4. AMV/RA: Danny can't go, but Fran can. Fran can go, but Danny can't go.
200

**DAY 54**:  1.  Dear, Ann, I    2.  Tony, are you sad?    3.  AMV/RA:  large, huge
4.  AMV/RA:  The deer heard a noise and looked around.  When the deer heard a noise, it looked around.

**DAY 55**:  1.  Their, Saturday, July    2.  Linda shared candy, nuts, and chips.
3.  not safe    4.  AMV/RA:  Those chips and this bread are stale.

**DAY 56**:  1.  My, I, Phoenix, Zoo    2.  Jill's necklace has eighty-two pearls.
3.  adjective    4.  AMV/RA:  Tate wants to go to the library, but nobody can take him.  Although Tate wants to go to the library, nobody can take him.

**DAY 57**:  1.  Their, Peoria, Sports, Complex    2.  dog's    3.  sounds
4.  AMV/RA:  Miss Smith smiled and handed me a paper.  Miss Smith smiled as she handed me a paper.  As Miss Smith handed me a paper, she smiled.

**DAY 58**:  1.  Have, Firebird, Stadium    2.  cart's    3.  statement    4.  AMV/RA:
The coach handed Sue and Adam each a trophy.

**DAY 59**:  1.  The, Farm    2.  No, the bus won't stop here.    3.  They (*We* is also
acceptable if a boy perceives a reference to himself and others.)    4.  AMV/RA:  This floor is very clean and shiny.  This clean floor is very shiny.  This very shiny floor is clean.  This floor is very shiny because it is clean.  Because the floor is clean, it is very shiny.

**DAY 60**:  1.  She, Sleeping, Beauty    2.  The red juicy apples weren't in the
basket.  3.  a) apple  b) card  c) fast  d) flat  e) heart    4.  AMV/RA:  Peter's cow won a ribbon at the fair yesterday.  Yesterday, Peter's cow won a ribbon at the fair.

**DAY 61**:  1.  Is, Mummy, Mountain, Arizona    2.  That large brown hen won't lay
eggs.  3.  kindly    4.  AMV/RA:  Maria wrote a story about two monsters.

**DAY 62**:  1.  John, I, Broken, Arrow    2.  Three black horses are in the field.
3.  brush, sink    4.  AMV/RA:  Forks, knives, and spoons are on the table.

**DAY 63**:  1.  Has , Micah, Otter, World    2.  Dear Jay,    3.  and (or)
4.  AMV/RA:  Max loves shrimp salad, but his sisters don't like it.  Although Max loves shrimp salad, his sisters do not.

**DAY 64**:  1.  On, Memorial, Day, New, York    2.  friend's    3.  <u>cows</u>
4.  AMV/RA:  We cheered for my brother's team, but the other team won.  Although we cheered for my brother's team, the other team won.

**DAY 65**:  1.  Your, Carli    2.  Wow!  I've nearly hit the target!    3.  ate
4.  AMV/RA:  They are drawing pictures with chalk.  They are using chalk to draw pictures.

**DAY 66**:  1.  See, Wendy   2.  Bill's   3.  washed   4.  AMV/RA: Our friends are baking cookies for a bake sale.

**DAY 67**:  1.  Cody's, Bell, Street, Reno, NV   2.  a) girl's  b) jar's  3. a) Yeah! b) Wow!   4.  AMV/RA:  I built a birdhouse, but my mother helped me.  My mother helped me build a birdhouse.  My mother and I built a birdhouse.

**DAY 68**:  1.  Is, Lake, Champlain, Canada   2.  a) <u>Ira Sleeps Over</u>  b) "The Cat's Purr"   3. and (or)   4.  AMV/RA: Mark's cat sleeps with him.  Mark has a cat that sleeps with him.

**DAY 69**:  1.  Dear, Koko, I'll, Hugs, Anna   2.  a) <u>The Red Cloak</u>   b) "The Story of a Young Artist"   3.  toothbrush   4.  AMV/RA:  Ada and Lexa play school.

**DAY 70**:  1.  We, Salt, River, Friday, August   2.  Our flag is red, white, and blue.   3.  statement   4.  AMV/RA: A plumber fixes sinks and toilets.  A plumber fixes both sinks and toilets.

**DAY 71**:  1.  Dear, Rick, In, Skunk, Creek, Your, Maddy   2.  They'll be thirty years old on Jan. 12, 2020.   3.  AMV/RA:  a) for the meeting   b) to France  4.  AMV/RA:  Jacy fell off a hay wagon, but he was not hurt.  When Jason fell off the wagon, he was not hurt.  Jason was not hurt when he fell off the wagon.

**DAY 72**:  1.  Last, Miss, Motts, Hawaii   2.  pigs'   3. a) hap py   b) mom  4.  AMV/RA:  After Mrs. Fay goes to the library, she will go to the store.  Mrs. Fay will go to the store after she goes to the library.  Mrs. Fay is going first to the library and then to the store.

**DAY 73**:  1.  Do, English   2.  boys'   3.  dog, ham, boat   4.  AMV/RA:  Dave and Jill have gone to visit a sick friend.  Jill has gone with Dave to visit a sick friend.

**DAY 74**:  1.  Miss, Bota, What   2.  A small child cried, "Where is my momma?"  3.  gently   4.  AMV/RA: The chocolate cake has white frosting with pink sprinkles.

**DAY 75**:  1.  Mark, How   2.  Nick said, "Our car has a flat tire."   3.  Yes  4.  AMV/RA:  Joy likes carrots, corn, and green beans.

**DAY 76**:  1.  The, France, French   2.  They're reading <u>Bubble Bubble</u>.  3.  AMV/RA:  bad, difficult   4.  AMV/RA:  Tate and I have snowball fights and · sled in the winter.

**DAY 77**:  1.  We, Dover, General, Hospital   2.  Miss Jones, may we read?  3.  Four (classes), many (songs)   4.  AMV/RA:  They have to clean their messy room.  They have to clean their room because it is a mess.

202

**DAY 78**:   1.  Her, Rangers, Club     2.  Yes, I'm going with you.    3.  She
4.  AMV/RA:  Cereal, pancakes, and eggs are breakfast foods.

**DAY 79**:   1.  Has, Mr., James, Young, Life     2.  The lamb's wool is white and
fluffy.    3.  there    4.  AMV/RA:  Jana swims, skis, and takes dance lessons.

**DAY 80**:   1.  Pott's, Grocery, Store, Virginia     2.  Nov. 30, 2015
3.  a) submarines   b) A submarine is an underwater boat.    4.  AMV/RA:
Leah cut her lip on this chipped cup.

**DAY 81**:   1.  My, Friendship, Club     2.  Friday, December 5, 2020    3.  adjective
4.  AMV/RA:  The clerk smiled and gave me change.  The clerk smiled as he
gave me change.  As the clerk gave me change, he smiled.

**DAY 82**:   1.  The, Brooklyn, Bridge, New, York     2.  La Quinta, CA  92253
3.  <u>artist</u> <u>painted</u>    4.  AMV/RA:  My grandpa walks two miles every day.

**DAY 83**:   1.  The, Thursday, Keys, Elementary, School     2.  a) <u>The Rainbow
Fish</u>          b) "Driving on Ice"    3.  doesn't    4.  AMV/RA:  Jason grinned
and hid his hands behind his back.  While Jason grinned, he hid his hands
behind his back.

**DAY 84**:   1.  His, Treasure, Island     2.  AMV/RA: CT    3.  a)  wouldn't
b) I've   c) here's   d) you'll    4.  AMV/RA:  Tommy runs faster than Bart
or Jenny.

**DAY 85**:   1.  On, Presidents', Day, Colorado, River     2.  a) girl's   b)  girls'
3.  a) I'm   b) aren't   c) who's   d) they're    4.  AMV/RA:  Jacy is making a
black bracelet for his brother.  Jacy is making his brother a black bracelet.

**DAY 86**:   1.  Rusty's, Sky, Diner     2.  a) nurse's   b) nurses'    3.  a) statement
b) command     4.  AMV/RA:  The streetlights have come on because it is dark.
Because it is dark, the streetlights have come on.

**DAY 87**:   1.  Did, Mrs., A., Vargas     2.  Little Rock, AR  72201    3.  a)  student's
name   b) I    4.  AMV/RA:  I am taking a raft to the beach.

**DAY 88**:   1.  Is, Hope, Church, Daisy, Drive     2.  He lives at 102 S. Mill Lane,
Lubbock, TX  79493.    3.  AMV/RA: Hurrah!    4.  AMV/RA:  They are cutting
out stars and flowers for their scrapbook.

**DAY 89**:   1.  May, Parks, Mall     2.  a) squirrel's   b)  squirrels'    3.  a) cooks
b) cooked    4.  AMV/RA:  We had fun ice skating on a pond.

**DAY 90**:  1.  A, Bahama, Islands, September
2.   Dear Tim,
      You're a good friend.
          Your pal,
          Ron
3.  a)  student's name   b)  me    4.  AMV/RA:  When Fran opened the door, her
puppy ran out.

**DAY 91**:  1.  Upside, Down    2.  His sister will marry at 2:00 in Lutz, Florida.
3.  student's name, my    4.  AMV/RA:  mad    5.  AMV/RA:  Jana and her
brother like to hike.

**DAY 92**:  1.  !s, Oakwood, College, Dale, Street    2.  He knows that you're
here.  3.  them    4.  command    5.  AMV/RA:  Matt and his sister play
soccer.

**DAY 93**:  1.  Has, Aunt, Kate, Jacob's, Ladder    2.  The party will start at 6:30
on Saturday, July 13.    3. a)  peaches  b)  pears  c)  slushes   d)  boxes
4.  fast   5.  AMV/RA:  Tara's ball is red with a wide blue stripe.

**DAY 94**:  1.  Did, Grandma, Liss, The, Rainbow, Fish    2.  Jill's scooter is
yellow and black.   3.  fast   4. a)  banana   b)  deer   c)  elk   d)  lamb
5.  AMV/RA:  Kim is washing and waxing his truck.

**DAY 95**:  1.  We, English    2.  Dora asked, "Will you hold this?"   3.  furry
(kitten), soft (blanket)    4.  his    5.  AMV/RA:  Carli is making meat loaf,
mashed potatoes, and peas for dinner.

**DAY 96**:  1.  Last, Captain, Bree, Scotland    2.  Have you ever been to Buffalo,
New York?   3.  anything    4.  looked    5.  AMV/RA:  Kala ate eggs, toast,
and ham for breakfast.

**DAY 97**:  1.  During, Naco, School, Mexico    2.  They met on Friday, March 31,
2006.    3. a)  tiny (dog)  b)  log (house)   4. a)  sticks   b)  ranches
5.  AMV/RA:  Todd picked up a stone and threw it into the creek.  After Todd
picked up a stone, he threw it into the creek.

**DAY 98**:  1.  They, Ellis, Park, Labor, Day    2. a)  uncle's  b)  uncles'
3. a)  can't   b)  where's   c)  I'll  d)  wasn't    4. Birds <u>fly</u>
5.  AMV/RA:  Do you want a glass of milk and a banana for a snack?

**DAY 99**:  1.  Did, Aunt, Koko, United, States, Gateway, College    2.  Josh
asked, "Did Mom run errands today?"   3.  anything    4.  likes    5.  AMV/RA:
The man waved and stood up.  As the man waved, he stood up.

**DAY 100**:   1.  Are, Uncle, Tom, I, Christmas     2.  Haven't you eaten tiny green peas?   3.  later   4.  skated   5.  AMV/RA:  Paco bought a bowling ball for his sister.

**DAY 101**:   1.  The, Red, Hat, Society, Thursday     2.  Wow!  Both of my sisters' artwork won blue ribbons!   3.  a) person - dad   b) place - rodeo   4.  a) want   b) wanted     5.  AMV/RA:  Their black iron gate is heavy.  Their heavy black gate is made of iron.

**DAY 102**:   1.  Pam, I, Smokey, Mountains, Tennessee     2.  No, our dog doesn't bite.   3.  will stop   4.  hallway   5.  AMV/RA:  Katy's mom has a yellow truck with blue stripes.

**DAY 103**:   1.  Dear, Mike, I, Your, Bo   2.  a) "When the Clock Was Sick"   b) <u>If I Had a Gorilla</u>   3.  happy   4.  rips   5.  AMV/RA:  Dark clouds rolled in, and it began to rain.  When dark clouds rolled in, it began to rain.

**DAY 104**:   1.  Is, Lake, Pleasant, Pacific, Ocean   2.  Dear Fred, / Your friend,   3.  anything   4.  stands   5.  AMV/RA:  This velvet pillow has tiny purple buttons.

**DAY 105**:   1.  His, Oak, Mountain, State, Park, Pelham, Alabama     2.  Yuck!  Their dog has fleas!   3.  these (cups); that (box)   4.  a) mole   b) open   c) ship   d) tale   5.  AMV/RA:  An emu is a bird that lays eggs, but it cannot fly.  Although an emu is a bird that can't fly, it lays eggs.

**DAY 106**:   1.  Their, Coe, Street, November     2.  Miss Carr, may we pass out papers?   3.  AMV/RA:  a) in the attic   b) from the ship   4.  fan, share, drill   5.  AMV/RA:  This milk tastes bad because it is sour.  This sour milk tastes bad.  Because this milk is sour, it tastes bad.

**DAY 107**:   1.  In, January, Italy   2.  toddlers'   3.  AMV/RA:  front   4.  <u>Cows eat</u>   5.  AMV/RA:  Beavers do not live in Florida or Mexico.

**DAY 108**:   1.  Dr., Mrs., Cobb, Yellowstone, National, Park   2.  Mrs. Diaz lives at 22 East Woods Dr., Saline, MI  48176.   3.  AMV/RA:  a) of sugar   b) at the zoo   4.  AMV/RA:  fame   5.  AMV/RA:  Molly likes to ski, but she does not like to skate.   Although Molly likes to ski, she does not like to skate.

**DAY 109**:   1.  Has, Dr., Jacobs, Brookside, Gardens, Wheaton, Maryland   2.  No, I don't want pie, cake, or pudding.   3.  a) grape   b) harp   c) ink   d) king   4.  make   5.  AMV/RA:  My friend laughed, and tears rolled down her cheeks.  As my friend laughed, tears rolled down her cheeks.

**DAY 110**: 1. Our, Aunt, Jo, Moss, School 2. "Are you ready?" asked Ann.
3. soon 4. <u>Bats</u> <u>fly</u> 5. AMV/RA: A raccoon has a chunky body, a broad head, and a bushy tail.

**DAY 111**: 1. Our, Columbus, Day
2. Beth R. Parker
   12 N. Ash Street
   Moore, OK 73160
3. a) you're b) don't c) isn't d) they'll 4. nonstop
5. AMV/RA: Alligators live only in China or in the United States.

**DAY 112**: 1. Have, London, Bridge 2. She was given a grey coat, a black cape, and a white hat. 3. Yes 4. They're 5. AMV/RA: Micah, Jenny, and Peter want to ski soon.

**DAY 113**: 1. a) The, Golden, Egg b) Gulp, Lion 2. Sam, will you read me the book named <u>Professor Wormbug</u>? 3. Several (kittens), one (pillow)
4. a) It's b) Their 5. AMV/RA: Kirk broke eggs into a bowl, and Marco beat them. After Kirk broke eggs into a bowl, Marco beat them.

**DAY 114**: 1. They, Phoenix, Suns
2. Mr. Fred Smith
   12 Green Apple Ave.
   Dallas, Texas 75214
3. coin, table 4. or (and) 5. AMV/RA: Carla bought a glass music box.

**DAY 115**: 1. I, Bear, Island, Lake, Superior 2. Jimmy's cousin didn't take his picture. 3. (brown) bugs, (tall) grass 4. a) <u>A</u> b) <u>A</u> c) _
5. AMV/RA: Goose Lake is close to Egg Lake in Canada.

**DAY 116**: 1. My, Star, Dance, Club 2. a) gerbil's b) gerbils'
3. a) command b) question 4. doesn't 5. AMV/RA: Jacob lost his gold ring with a small red stone.

**DAY 117**: 1. Does, Dr., Martin, Dallas, Children's, Hospital 2. Danny's dad made salad, pasta, and garlic bread. 3. AMV/RA: *at* her house 4. right
5. AMV/RA: Joe cut himself and needs a bandage. Joe needs a bandage because he cut himself. Because Joe cut himself, he needs a bandage.

**DAY 118**: 1. They, Vera, Beach, August 2. Tuesday, May 15, 2007
3. <u>Ann</u> <u>goes</u> ~~to the zoo~~ ~~with her class~~. 4. meat 5. AMV/RA: Her bike is a red racer. Her racing bike is red.

**DAY 119**:  1.  Have, Bulls, Bay, South, Carolina    2.  Yuck!  This tastes awful!
3.  A <u>rabbit</u> ~~with brown fur~~ <u>hopped</u> ~~to our patio~~.    4.  AMV/RA:  fun, love
5.  AMV/RA:  Sally is on the swimming and diving teams.  Sally is on both the
swimming team and the diving team.

**DAY 120**:  1.  The, Walnut, Valley, Festival, Winfield, Kansas    2.  Jacy's
brother hasn't moved to Reno, Nevada.    3.  too    4.  a)  benches   b)  dollars
c)  fizzes   d)  taxes    5.  AMV/RA:  Loni is angry because her brother won't let
her play.  Because Loni's brother won't let her play, she is angry.

**DAY 121**:  1.  Many, Philly, Fest, Philadelphia    2.  a) <u>Fancy Nancy</u>
b)  "I Bought a Pet Tomato"   c)  "My Dog Nicki"    3.  blonde (hair), blue (eyes);
(He <u>has</u>)    4.  walks    5.  AMV/RA:  Paco takes drum lessons from Miss Snow.
Miss Snow is teaching Paco to play drums.

**DAY 122**:  1.  Grandmother, Mills, Dulles, Airport    2.  Yippee!  We've won the
game!    3.  a) <u>A</u> (<u>horse</u> <u>runs</u>)    b)  _  (<u>You</u> <u>are</u>)    c) <u>A</u> (<u>She</u> <u>smiles</u>)
4.  AMV/RA:  sidewalk    5.  AMV/RA:  Nan dropped a dime, and Parker picked it
up.  Parker picked up the dime that Nan dropped.  When Nan dropped a dime,
Parker picked it up.

**DAY 123**:  1.  We, Rainbow, Natural, Bridge, Arizona
2.  Mrs. Sandy Barn
    98 Cotton Ln.
    Newton, NC   28658
3. <u>sister</u> <u>flosses</u>    4.  AMV/RA:  thin    5.  AMV/RA:  Jina and Peter are pitchers.
Both Jina and Peter are pitchers.

**DAY 124**:  1.  Dear, Linda, My, I, Love, Sarah    2.  I like juice, cereal, and toast
for breakfast.    3.  A, an    4.  a)  friends   b)  wishes   c)  feet
5.  AMV/RA:  Her skirt and blouse are blue.  Both her skirt and blouse are blue.

**DAY 125**:  1.  Has, Ron, Mt., Everest    2.  The dog's tail is black and white.
3.  question    4.  Jenny and I    5.  AMV/RA:  Tim is holding a tennis racket
that his uncle and aunt gave to him.  Tim is holding a tennis racket, a gift from
his aunt and uncle.  (This is appositive construction.)

**DAY 126**:  1.  Our, Coach, Car, Service, Ohio    2.  His pen, pencil, and pad are
on the couch.    3.  Mission Beach   4.  AMV/RA:  dime, rhyme    5.  AMV/RA:
Joy ran after a ball and fell over a chunk of wood.  When Joy ran after a ball, she
fell over a chunk of wood.

**DAY 127**:  1.  Do, South, Coast, Highway, Newport, Beach    2.  His baptism
was Sunday, Aug. 6, 2006.    3.  sing    4.  their    5.  AMV/RA:  Jacy and Jenny
live near an old mine.

**DAY 128**: 1. Did, Ms., Gregg, Cape, Cod, Massachusetts  2. They'll visit on Wednesday, January 17.  3. two  4. a) likes  b) like  5. AMV/RA: Bart's parents will take him to their doctor because he has a very sore throat.

**DAY 129**: 1. Last, I, England  2. a) st.  b) Sept.  c) in.  d) Sat.
3. anything  4. AMV/RA: Taffy  5. AMV/RA: Her bracelet is made of light green pebbles.

**DAY 130**: 1. Robby, How  2. No, his father's name isn't Harry.  3. friend's name; he or she  4. She waits ~~for her bus by a mailbox~~.  5. AMV/RA: Miss Jackson smiled as she handed me a ribbon.  Miss Jackson smiled and handed me a ribbon.  Smiling, Miss Jackson handed me a ribbon.

**DAY 131**: 1. The, French, Lewes, Beach, Atlantic, Ocean  2. Dave, Sue, and Don arrived at 8 o'clock.  3. here, quietly  4. model smiled
5. AMV/RA: A komodo dragon is a lizard that can grow to three meters long. A komodo dragon, a lizard, can grow to three meters long.

**DAY 132**: 1. Our, Payson, Country, Music, Festival  2. They're meeting the salon's owner at 12:30.  3. ~~After the game~~, people talked ~~to both coaches~~.
4. deeper, tonight, candle  5. AMV/RA:  This metal bat has a baseball player's name on it.

**DAY 133**: 1. We, Glendale, Public, Library  2. Peter will be twenty-seven on Thursday, Feb. 28.  3. doesn't  4. He types  5. AMV/RA: Hannah was born in France, but her family has moved to Utah.  Although Hannah was born in France, her family has moved to Utah.

**DAY 134**: 1. Ella, My, Mama, Bear, Preschool  2. Have you read Castle?
3. chew  4. a) lace  b) limb  c) loan  d) rabbit  5. AMV/RA: Nicky and Terry have dirty hands because they have been pulling weeds.  Because they have been pulling weeds, Nicky and Terry have dirty hands*.
*Introducing various sentence structures is a good idea.

**DAY 135**: 1. My, When, I, Always, Ray  2. There are twenty-one forks and thirty-nine knives in this drawer.  3. a) boy's  b) doll's  c) girl's  4. here
5. AMV/RA: The chair is purple with pink stripes.

**DAY 136**: 1. Our, Uncle, Fred, Mexico  2. Salem, Oregon  3. A herd ~~of cattle~~ roamed ~~in the meadow~~.  4. AMV/RA: Cool!  5. AMV/RA: Her hair is wet, her eyes are red, and her lips are turning blue.

**DAY 137**: 1. Yesterday, Fairview, Bowling, Alley  2. Yes, it's now 2:00.
3. student's name – I  4. a) reheat  b) heat again  5. AMV/RA: The chocolate birthday cake has orange icing.

**DAY 138**:   1.  Did, Miss, Borg, Charlotte's, Web
2.    Michael A. Hall
      57 Linx Ave.
      Tulsa, OK   74133
3.    North Sea   4.  You're   5.  AMV/RA: When the taxi driver slowed, a lady crossed the street.  The taxi driver slowed for a lady to cross the street.  The taxi driver slowed as a lady crossed the street.

**DAY 139**: 1.  Her, The, Cat, Joey   2.  Ben, may I go with you?    3.  sick
4.  Her <u>cat</u> <u>purred</u> softly.    5.  AMV/RA: We will put food into this large bag.  We will put food into this bag because it is large.  Because this bag is large, we will put food into it.

**DAY 140**:  1.  Tomorrow, I, Herbie, Rides, Again    2.  We arrived at 10:30 on Friday, Oct. 23.    3.  25   4.  Pretty (flowers), maple (tree)   5.  AMV/RA: During the storm, lightning flashed, and thunder boomed.  Lightning flashed, and thunder boomed during the storm.  (Technically, a comma isn't needed when connecting two short sentences [independent clauses].)

**DAY 141**:   1.  Janet, Gobb, Lake, Erie   2.  Sandy, have you read the book, <u>Half of an Elephant</u>? 3.  ball, sofa   4. Yes    5.  AMV/RA: Jack wants pizza for lunch, but Jana wants a tuna salad.  Although Jack wants pizza for lunch, Jana wants a tuna salad.

**DAY 142**:  1.  Dear, Anna, Come, Love, Betsy   2.  Orlando, Florida
3. a) babies  b) boys   4.  our    5.  AMV/RA: Their sister, who likes to skate,* is thirteen.   Their thirteen-year-old sister likes to skate.
*This sentence without commas is also acceptable.

**DAY 143**:  1.  Did, Niagara, Falls, New, York   2.  The play will be Tuesday, Feb. 4.    3.  from Grandma   4.  AMV/RA: cook, took   5.  AMV/RA:  Their grammy, who lives in Delaware,* has blue eyes and blonde hair.
*This sentence without commas is also acceptable.

**DAY 144**:   1.  Mr., John, I., Sarter, North, Maple, Street, Upper, Saddle, River, NJ  2.  A cow's tail is very long.    3.  <u>re</u> + <u>paint</u> + <u>ing</u>  4.  Yes
5.  AMV/RA:  Snow has fallen, and everyone is sledding.   Everyone is sledding because snow has fallen.   Because snow has fallen, everyone is sledding.

**DAY 145**:  1.  The, Jillian, Jigs, Phoebe, Gilman   2.  Ann, have you seen these girls' mother?   3.   a) ladder  b) lift  c) pony  d) up   4. a) keys
b) bunnies   5.  AMV/RA: The oak chest belongs to Mrs. Karn.   The chest that is oak belongs to Mrs. Karn.   Mrs. Karn's chest is oak.

**DAY 146:**  1.  An, America, Mayfair, School    2.  a) ft.   b) yd.  c) Dr.
3.  <u>chews</u>    4.  The (group), an (inn), a (village)    5.  AMV/RA:  Larry's favorite
dessert is berry pie, but my favorite dessert is fruit salad.  Although Larry's
favorite dessert is berry pie, my favorite desert is fruit salad.

**DAY 147:**  1.  I.  Flowers
                     II.  Trees and bushes
2.  Joe said, "Look here."    3.  a) C   b) P   c) C   d) P    4.  AMV/RA:  pack
5.  AMV/RA:   Jana's knee, ankle, and foot are sore.

**DAY 148:**  1.  We, Independence, Day, July    2.  Sarah asked, "Are you sure?"
3.  shorter    4.  late, tomorrow    5.  AMV/RA:  The leaves have changed color
because it is autumn.  Because it is autumn, the leaves have changed color.

**DAY 149:**  1.  Dear, Mrs., Winston, We, Sunday, November, Your, Lucy
2.  David's dad was born on Oct. 12, 1965.    3.  126   4.  <u>aunt</u> <u>drives</u>
5.  AMV/RA:  A squirrel gathers and stores nuts for the winter.

**DAY 150:**  1.  a) Bunnicula   b) Jack, Beanstalk    2.  They haven't been to
Dade City, Florida.    3.  46    4.  sub    5.  AMV/RA:  After Jana played soccer,
she went to a music store.  Jana played soccer and then went to a music store.

**DAY 151:**  1.  Was, President, Madison, United, States    2.  Yeah!  Let's go!
3.  a) It's  b) too    4.  keys, dentist, Texas    5.  AMV/RA:  Mrs. Cod and her
daughter work in the same card shop.

**DAY 152:**  1.  The, Brooks, Flathead, Lake, Idaho   2.  Kim, you're a good football and
tennis player.   3.  Some small red (cherries); a tin (bucket)  4.  <u>washed</u>; <u>dried</u>
5.  AMV/RA:  Misha paints and sells animal pictures.  The pictures that Misha paints and
sells are of animals.

**DAY 153:**  1.  a) Noah's, Ark    b) Lost, Horizon
2.   I. Trees
         A.  Birch
         B.  Pine
     II. Bushes
3.  a) taller   b) tallest    4.  a) or   b) and   c) but    5.  AMV/RA:  A mountain
goat is standing high on a cliff.

**DAY 154:**  1.  Their, Park, Lane   2.  a) "The Crocodile's Toothache"
b) "Sleeping Beauty"  c) <u>Mrs. Pigglewiggle</u>   3.  AMV/RA:  a)  Paula's Purses
b) Laura Bush   4.  a) strays   b) berries    5.  AMV/RA:  Zoey sanded and
stained her living room floor. Zoey sanded and stained the floor in her living
room.

**DAY 155**: 1. During, Senator, Owens, Dallas, Texas   2. We'll live at 12 Main Street, Atlanta, Georgia.   3. a) command - imperative  b) question - interrogative   4. she   5. AMV/RA: Take your papers from your backpack and give them to Ms. Dell.

**DAY 156**: 1. Is, Wayne, National, Forest, Ohio   2. a) Sat.  b) Ave.  c) Dec. d) qt.   3. around (where); later (when)   4. Yuck!   5. AMV/RA: Starvine Ranch is a working ranch where horses are raised.  Horses are raised on Starvine Ranch, a working ranch*.   *This is an appositive construction, but it's worth introducing.

**DAY 157**: 1. Has, Uncle, Mack, Anna   2. Her new address is 203 Frog Avenue, Highland Park, Illinois.   3. a) and   b) but   c) or   d) and (or) 4. baker, helper   5. AMV/RA: When the movie began, everyone took a seat. Everyone took a seat when the movie began.  Everyone took a seat because the movie began.  Because the movie began, everyone took a seat.

**DAY 158**: 1. a) Good, Boy, Fergus   b) Ella, Sarah, Gets, Dressed   c) A, Chair, My, Mother   2. Yes, we're giving Trena's friend a balloon.  3. anything 4. a) waved  b) sang   5. AMV/RA: As the basketball team ran onto the court, the fans cheered.  The fans cheered when the basketball team ran onto the court.  When the basketball team ran onto the court, the fans cheered.

**DAY 159**: 1. Dr., A., J., Smith, A   2. That pen's stripes are red, blue, and green.   3. a) chewed  b) sat   4. a) buses   b) papers   c) puppies d) mice   5. AMV/RA:  5. Troy sent a Valentine's card to his wife.

**DAY 160**: 1. Does, Lee, Spanish, Deep, River, School   2. a) Sun.  b) Rd. c) Aug.  d) ft.   3. with her friends, to the store   4. a) greeting   b) message or body  c) closing  d) signature   5. AMV/RA: The bright light shines in my window.

**DAY 161**: 1. We, Mississippi, River, Fran
2.                     111 East Brell Dr.
                       Atlantic City,  NJ
                       March 3, 20—

Dear Miss Than,
     Yes, I will come at 8:45.
                    Love,
                    Mandy
3. quite (active), so (funny)   4. your   5. AMV/RA: David is moving to New York next spring.

**DAY 162**: 1. a) The, Stray, Dog   b) The, Army, Two   c) Family, Circle
d) Make, Way, Wanda   2. Mandy's small brown dog isn't a bulldog.
3. but (possibly *and*)   4. <u>man</u>, <u>partner</u>   5. AMV/RA: Dreena twirls her
baton as she marches in a band.

**DAY 163**: 1. In, July, Merrimac, Caverns
2.                            678 Johnson St.
                             Gettysburg, PA  17325
                             February 7, 2009
Dear Ms. Little,
        Our plane will arrive at 2:15.
                             Truly yours,
                             Koko
3. date   4. AMV/RA: bottom   5. AMV/RA:  Sissy likes to swing at the park's
playground.  Sissy likes to swing at the playground at the park.

**DAY 164**: 1. Joy, J., Jones, Penn, Middle, School   2. Miss Clegg exclaimed,
"You are the winner!"   3. <u>driver</u> <u>yelled</u>   4. a) coaches   b) fences
c) baggies d) bays   5. AMV/RA:  Their scout troop will meet on Monday at
Marco's house.

**DAY 165**: 1. Is, North, America   2. A tall, famous arch is in St. Louis,
Missouri. 3. Yes   4. a) good  b) well   5. AMV/RA:  The cookies burned
because they were in the oven too long.  Because the cookies were in the oven
too long, they burned.

**DAY 166**: 1. North, Allen, Drive, Lubbock, TX, June, Dear, Aunt, Carole,
2. His three cousins' scooter is broken.   3. does*n't*   4. neat, messy
5. AMV/RA:  Some energetic puppies were playing together.

**DAY 167**: 1. The, Rangers', Club, South, Mountain, Fairgrounds   2. a) <u>Stone
Fox</u> b) "The Lost Colony"  c) <u>Animal Fun</u>   3. <u>swan</u>, <u>duck</u>   4. a) ba by
b) Sat ur day   5. AMV/RA:  His first airplane flight was to Denver, Colorado.

**DAY 168**: 1. The, Spanish, Mexico, City, July   2. A small, peppy puppy licked
its paws.  3. any   4. a) She or He   b) They   5. AMV/RA: Lacy bought a
pin for her mom, a pen for her dad, and a toy for her brother.

**DAY 169**: 1. Is, Everglades, National, Park, Florida   2. a) <u>Submarines</u>
b) "Lions and Tigers"  c) "Our Muscles"   3. a) went  b) will go
4. command (imperative)   5. AMV/RA:  Chan likes to play football, but he does
not like to run laps.  Although Chan likes to play football, he does not like to run
laps.

**DAY 170**:   1.  Their, We're, Mummasburg, Baseball, Festival   2. a) The Contest   b) "My Bug"   c) "Yankee Doodle"   3. a) This/That   b) these/those   4. a) children   b) teeth   c) moose   5. AMV/RA: We blew up balloons for Jimmy's first birthday party.

**DAY 171**:   1.  Will, Mr., Mrs., Cline, Morro, Bay     2.  Chan asked, "Aren't Rick, Frisco, and Jacy coming?"   3. 89   4. a) RV   b) IV   c) RV   d) IV   5. AMV/RA: Bert slipped on a banana peel, and he grabbed onto the counter. When Bert slipped on a banana peel, he grabbed onto the counter.

**DAY 172**:   1.  Will, Milton, Hospital, Tuesday    2.  We can't be next, Chris.   3. a) 2   b) 1   c) 3    4. a) I'm   b) haven't   c) won't   d) he's   5. AMV/RA:  As Jane swam across the pool, she yelled to her brother.

**DAY 173**:   1.  Was, Ms., Marks, L., D., Metro, Company   2.  Mr. Johns asked, "Where's the scouring pad?"    3. AMV/RA: a) Abraham Lincoln   b) Ty's Food Mart   4.  4    5. AMV/RA:  When Sammy jerked the reins, his horse reared back.  Because Sammy jerked the reins, his horse reared back.  Sammy's horse reared back because he jerked the reins.

**DAY 174**:   1.  Puddles, Not    2. a) U. S.   b) E.   c) Ln.   d) Dr.   3. a) everywhere   b) slowly   c) always    4. Two new blue (hats), a (chair)   5.  AMV/RA:  The White House is on Pennsylvania Avenue in Washington, D. C.

**DAY 175**:   1.   First, Then
2.  I.  Animal homes
        A.  Mountain animals
        B.  Desert animals
     II.  Animal food
3. a) fences   b) brushes   c) cups   d) rubies   e) mice   f) trays
4.  AMV/RA: very, rather    5.  AMV/RA:  Kari is wearing two pairs of socks because her toes are cold.  Because Kari's toes are cold, she is wearing two pairs of socks.

**DAY 176**:   1.  We, Hoover, Dam, Boulder, City    2.  Put Jonah's pants, socks, and shirts into the washer.   3.  Zoey and I    4. a) three   b) under   5.  AMV/RA:  Their  cocker spaniel wears sweaters in the winter.

**DAY 177**:   1.  Is, St., Patrick's, Day, March    2. a) "Jack and Jill"   b) Rosa   c) "Lemonade Stand"   3.  a) They're   b) Two   c) any    4. a) bend   b) brim   c) brook   d) cart   e) draw    5. AMV/RA: Jacy will sleep in his new tent tonight.

1. Sally, Founders', Day, Rodeo     2. Pat lives at 20 Dree Drive, California 93907.   3. a) past   b) future   c) present     4. a) larger est   5. AMV/RA: The winner is Susie, my neighbor.

**179**:   1. You, Northridge, Community, Church, Dynamite, Road Lana's mom exclaimed, "You did well!"     3. Those <u>flowers</u> <u>bloom</u> ~~in late~~ ~~spring~~.   4. a) drank   b) rode   c) gone   d) bought   5. AMV/RA: Uncle Luke bought his wife a silver charm bracelet.  Uncle Luke bought his wife a charm bracelet that is silver.

**DAY 180**:   1. Jenny, May, I, American     2. Jim's address is 22 Maple Street, Rembert, South Carolina  29128.   3. Her <u>aunt</u> ~~from Florida~~ <u>arrived</u> ~~at the~~ ~~airport~~.   4. 33-37     5. AMV/RA: Micah was sick, but he wanted to go out to play.  Although Micah was sick, he wanted to go out to play.